W9-BRI-142

The CAFE Book

The CAFE Book

Engaging All Students in Daily Literacy Assessment & Instruction

GAIL BOUSHEY & JOAN MOSER
"The Sisters"

STENHOUSE PUBLISHERS
PORTLAND, MAINE

PEMBROKE PUBLISHERS
MARKHAM, ONTARIO

Stenhouse Publishers
www.stenhouse.com

Pembroke Publishers
www.pembrokepublishers.com

Library of Congress Cataloging-in-Publication Data
Boushey, Gail, 1956–
The CAFE book : engaging all students in daily literacy assessment and instruction / Gail Boushey and Joan Moser.
p. cm.
ISBN 978-1-57110-728-2 (alk. paper)
1. Language arts—Ability testing. 2. Reading—Ability testing. I. Moser, Joan, 1962– II. Title.
LB1576.B533 2009
372.6'046—dc22

2008054539

Cover design, interior design, and typesetting by Martha Drury
Photographs by Jim Whitney, Lori Sabo, and Sonja Entmark
Manufactured in the United States of America on acid-free, recycled paper
15 14 13 12 11 10 09 9 8 7 6 5 4

Dedicated to . . .

Marilyn, Guy, Carol, and Dan, for helping us become who we are;

Jolie, Emily, and Madeline, for your wonderful personalities, love for each other, and joie de vivre;

Dean and Doug, for your support from home or while on the road;

Marlene, for your love of learning, zest for new ideas, and unconditional mother's love;

and

Dad, the wisest man we know and the best dad we could imagine.

Contents

Acknowledgments

The work behind this book was our passion even before our first book was published. Whereas *The Daily Five* established the core structural environment and the capacity for independence to meet the needs of our diverse students, *The CAFE Book* provides the technical expertise necessary for individual students to receive exactly what they need to improve as readers. Such an undertaking requires a huge supporting cast, all of whom deserve our deepest thanks for their ideas, support, and courage to develop the ideas in this book.

Richard Allington has inspired us the most. His vision gives us the energy to pinpoint how effective instruction is the only avenue to give all students what they need.

Regie Routman's words have always influenced us. Her warmth, encouragement, and interest have been a source of strength for us.

Meridian Elementary embodies all of the elements for a successful school: building and teacher leadership, collaboration, and a commitment to improve. Stan, Janet, Heather, Pam, Kelly, Kaye, Christie, Daniel, Cindy, Camille, Courtney, Kristen, Steve, Tiffany, Cathie, Carla, Ashley, Donna, Trina, Lucy, Jill, Ron, Jenny, Kathy, Mary, Patti, Sherry, Chris, Alene, Ann, Marie, Keith, Esther, and Dave—you guys are great.

The staff at Green Gables has provided the nurturing environment to seek new ways to meet the needs of all kids. Diane, Tod, Jenna, Teresa, Lindy, Carrie, Natalie, Marianne, Kim, Sharon, Hazel, Wendy, Alisha, Christine, Angela, Diane, Patty, Amy, Jen, Anhsaly, Dana, Kris, Karen, Evan, and Kristen—we appreciate you.

Our Sunrise friends were early implementers who have gone on to enrich the lives of students in many places: Steve, Pam, Anne, Melissa, Kristi, Wendy, Jaime, and Janet.

Janet Scott and Heidi Smith are the best teaching partners we could ask for—collaborative, smart, and kind. Everything is so easy when working with them.

Susannah Klovdahl, the most efficient and organized person we know, brings constant support to us.

Lori Sabo's humor, wit, and creative thinking are special gifts to us. When an alternative approach is needed, she is flexible, accessible, and reliable.

The staff at Stenhouse Publishers have believed in us and provided us with tremendous support. Philippa Stratton, Bill Varner, Nate Butler, Jay Kilburn, Chris Downey, and the rest of the gang—a million thanks.

Martha Drury, who designed this book as well as many other projects, always makes us look good.

Brenda Power's brilliant vision, synthesizing skills, gift-giving creativity, and humor enrich us professionally and personally every day. She is a "dream" editor and cherished friend.

Jolie, Emily, and Madeline make us proud, and we appreciate your kind interest in our projects.

Dean and Doug's humor, patience, support, and encouragement help us pursue the work we love.

And finally, in appreciation of all the educators who have joined us through book studies, blogs, conversations, conferences, and classes—it is with colleagues such as you that we are able to reflect and refine our craft of teaching far beyond what we could possibly do alone.

Thank you!

Chapter 1

Introduction: The Beginnings of the CAFE Menu Assessment System

A confession: even though this is a research-based guide and system, we didn't create it while we were in school. The inspiration came when we were on a beach, talking about our frustrations with our reading programs. Because let's face it: even when we're on vacation, most of us who teach don't really get away from the problems or issues that are nagging at us.

At the beach, we chatted about assessment, skills we were teaching, and how little follow-through we seemed to have with students after connecting the two. We would teach strategies and put them up on a bulletin board, and they'd stay in front of us, but students didn't access them. The instruction was random, with little order or organization to help us or our students sort through what the strategies meant to them, or how they fit into their own progress or needs as readers.

Finally, we started thinking, "Well, what kind of skills are they?" There on the sand, we realized that all the skills we were teaching our children would fit under the headings of Comprehension and Fluency, and that obviously, Accuracy would be essential for our emergent readers just cracking the code. The final category we came up with was Vocabulary, based on the research into what skills all proficient readers need. We named that category Expand Vocabulary because it would reflect our desire to help students build their vocabularies, and of course so that we would have a catchy acronym: Comprehension (C), Accuracy (A), Fluency (F), and Expand vocabulary (E). The acronym CAFE also reflects our desire to have a selection of choices, instead of a set, sequential order of skills arbitrarily assigned by someone who does not know our children.

The CAFE Menu of strategies reflects the skills we've researched and used in our own classrooms, but these are not the only strategies proficient readers use. We encourage our colleagues to use them as a starting point, the base of comprehension, accuracy, fluency, and expanding vocabulary. Others can be added that are important or required in your district or state. It's a flexible system that can be tailored to individual classrooms, schools, or districts.

Although the beginnings of the CAFE system may seem whimsical, the system has added a coherence and structure to our work with children that was lacking in previous years. It reflects our belief that different children have different needs as readers, but that all readers, regardless of age, need instruction and support that helps them become more independent and self-reflective in their work.

Assessment Systems: But for What?

Where We Came From: Gail's Story

I remember early in my career the humiliating experience of being so disorganized when I went to do an assessment of a child that I had to send him back to his seat without administering it. I called Joan and asked for advice on getting set up. The purpose of that particular assessment was to find out what reading level the child was at, long before running records were popular. After talking with Joan, I set up the assessment area on the counter in the classroom. The pens were ready, including my favorite black fine-point style so I could make all the miscue marks on the page and still be able to read them. I now had an assessment box, with neatly labeled file folders. I'd heard that 80 percent of what we do is based on how we look, and my assessment corner looked fantastic.

Now when I pulled the same boy over to assess him, I was comfortable, not scrambling to find my pen or the paper to fill out. I took copious notes, thinking that any little thing he said or did would help me. But I still had a nagging feeling I wasn't doing things right. Is this how other teachers took their notes? What did they do with the notes once they had them? Thank goodness the assessment was a basic reading inventory—practically "teacher-proof," as they said in those days. After the child read and I asked a few questions, I pulled out the little grid provided and was given a reading level based on the number of words read accurately and correct answers to the questions. It was all neat and tidy. Here was his level. But what was supposed to come next?

For years everyone we knew said our assessments should guide our instruction. Much of what we read focused on differentiating instruction. It made such sense to us, yet there was just one problem: exactly how were we to do that? We were very proficient at giving assessments, and we knew they were important for tracking student progress. However, taking our assessments to the next level of really knowing what kids needed to learn, and keeping all of the information organized in a concise, focused, and easy-to-use manner, stymied us.

We taught for a number of years in a school district that used a basal reading program. At that time the primary focus of the program was the delivery of content through whole-group instruction, with every child receiving the same reading strategies and the same instruction. Some of our kids were doing well, in particular those who always seemed to learn in spite of us. Many of our children were progressing, although not as fast as we thought they should or hoped they would. And then there were our most at-risk students, who were experiencing very little growth at all. These students were coming into our classrooms delayed, and our hope was to narrow that gap while they were with us. Instead we found the opposite to be true. The growth they were experiencing was not nearly enough to narrow the gap and let them catch up as the rest of the class progressed. If these students were making only minimal progress, we knew they would fall farther and farther behind with each passing year.

At the same time, we had been immersing ourselves in reading assessments and using those assessments to inform us of our children's strengths and greatest areas of need. The more we learned about our students, the more frustrated we became with our reading program. Here we had a classroom full of children, all with different needs and interests. Based on our assessments, we knew what our children were missing in their reading, yet we were teaching the whole group with a one-size-fits-all program—and they certainly were not all one size!

For some students the whole-group instruction was just what they needed so they could move forward in their reading. However, the majority of the class needed something completely different. As teachers we knew we needed to be able to meet with individuals and small groups without interruptions. But how could we keep the rest of the class engaged so we could conduct focused instruction in small groups as well as meet with children side by side to coach them?

It was at this point that the Daily Five was born (2006). The Daily Five system teaches children to work independently on five different tasks that they cycle through during literacy workshops: reading to self, reading to someone, writing, word work, and listening to reading. The Daily Five structure provided us with the time to meet with individuals and small groups while the rest of the class was engaged in meaningful and independent reading practice.

Daily Five was so successful in our classrooms that each day we were amazed at how independent our children were. We were thrilled with the extended amount of time our students now had to practice reading and writing, and we even began to see our kids making progress with all the extra practice time. We had ample time to work with kids in small groups. Even coaching our most struggling readers side by side was attainable.

Yet solving the problem of what to do with the rest of the class merely opened up a whole new set of issues in our teaching. These were our new questions:

- How do we organize all of our assessment data so we can make it work for us?
- How do we keep track of each child's strengths and goals so we can maximize our time with him or her?
- What about "flexible groups"? Is there really a way to make them flexible?
- How do we present strategies so that students can access them when needed and practice them until they are proficient?

CAFE is our answer to these issues that many teachers face. There are many excellent assessments available on the market, and we use some of them in our work with children, especially early in the year. But we never found anything that presented a practical, simple way to integrate assessment into the daily reading and discussions of our literacy workshops. CAFE is based on the most current research about developing proficient readers. It provides a vocabulary that teachers and students can share as they work together, set goals, and document learning and growth.

CAFE appeals to teachers because of its simplicity. It doesn't require a lot of expensive materials, complicated training, or a major upheaval of literacy workshop formats and routines. What it does is provide a structure for conferring, a language for talking about reading development, and a system for tracking growth and fostering student independence. We believe educators are always interested in new assessment systems because teachers have yet to find one that can be easily integrated into literacy workshops. CAFE addresses this need.

The Basics of CAFE Assessment

Where We Came From: Joan's Story

One late October early in my teaching career, I sat across the table from a particularly confrontational parent. It was conference time, and she was certain I was not aware of her "brilliant" daughter's skills and what to do to move her forward. The problem was, the parent was right. Her child was extremely bright, and I wasn't sure how best to help her.

The words from that mother stung. I went home and couldn't sleep. I had always been able to charm my way through any discussion with a parent—after all, I was famous in my family for being able to sell socks to a snake! I was devastated. I had a master's degree in reading and had studied work from researchers, but I didn't know how to assess a child to the point where I could move that child forward, regardless of his or her skill level. I knew I had to find better ways to figure out strengths as well as weaknesses so that I was serving the brightest children in the room as well as the strugglers.

In this age of accountability and increasing diversity, we need records that document how we are assisting each child with exactly the skills and instruction he or she needs. And now, when we teach a strategy and post it on the board in our classroom, children understand what it means and how it fits into their lives as readers.

The CAFE system is simple, with these core elements:

1. The teacher keeps a notebook with a few key record-keeping forms, including a calendar, individual student conference forms, and strategy group planners. We've included the templates (in the appendix), as well as sample completed forms (in the text), to help you get started.

The Conferring Notebook or "Pensieve" contains key forms.

2. Children meet with the teacher during literacy workshop conferences to be assessed, to receive focused, explicit instruction, to set goals, and then to follow up on progress. The teacher keeps track of progress on the goal sheet in the notebook and schedules the next conference on the calendar, and the child posts his or her goal on the class CAFE chart.

Kelly confers one on one.

3. The teacher plans small-group instruction based on clusters of students with similar needs in one of the CAFE categories. These groups are flexible, based on needs rather than reading levels. Often the teacher meets with groups of children who are reading different books at different levels but working on the same goal (such as fluency or expanding vocabulary).

Lori meets with a small group of students who are each reading a different book but working on the same strategy.

4. Whole-group instruction is based on needs that emerge for many children, often using texts from whole-class read-alouds or other shared materials.

Whole-group instruction: Heather teaches a comprehension strategy the majority of her class needs.

It's easiest to understand CAFE if you see it in action, which is why we've structured the book to include many examples of individual conferences, small groups based on each of the four CAFE components, and samples of whole-class lessons. Most of the book details the individual conferences linked to goals derived from the CAFE Menu; we spend far more time teaching children individually than we spend instructing the whole class as part of our CAFE system.

The Research Base for CAFE

The research base for CAFE began in graduate school, which we started early in our teaching careers. It was this educational process that opened our eyes and minds to the power of research and all the ways it could be applied practically in our classrooms. Awareness of current research gave us the courage to act on what we knew to be true even when it wasn't popular. We called these researchers our colleagues. They didn't know it, but Frank Smith, Michael Pressley, Richard Allington, Gerald Duffy, P. David Pearson, Ann McGill-Franzen, Margaret Mooney, and Regie Routman, to name a few, stood by us each day as we tried out their ideas behind the closed doors of our classrooms. We were under mandate to follow the scripts from our reading programs, but doing so went against what the researchers were saying worked best with children. It took more than courage in our earlier years to continue on this journey of going against those mandated programs. We supported each other with words of affirmation and kept our own data and research to document that what we were doing was working. Although we abandoned scripts early in our teaching, we have never lost the habit of taking notes, observing children closely, and making teaching decisions based on data. Perhaps this is the most enduring aspect of our teaching that these diverse researchers would all agree is best practice for any teacher.

CAFE is supported by research that goes back decades. We could start with Emmet Betts (1946), who spoke of matching readers with appropriate text that they can read independently. This strategy is found on the CAFE Menu under Fluency and our emphasis on students reading "good-fit books." Students must spend most of their day with material they can read.

We agree with the findings of Pressley (2006) and Taylor, Pearson, Clark, and Walpole (2000) that the more effective classrooms have a distribution of whole-class, small-group, and side-by-side instruction. The more whole-class teaching offered, the lower the academic achievement in any school. CAFE includes a system for managing grouping plans in our classrooms in a simple yet comprehensive way to ensure growth for all our students.

Diagnosing students' strengths and needs as readers and designing a path of instruction and practice for students is what we learned in our graduate studies in the disciplines of special education and reading. Looking back on Peter Johnston, Richard Allington, and Peter Afflerbach's work in an article titled "The Congruence of Classroom and Remedial Reading Instruction" (1985), we find this touchstone that has guided our work for more than two decades:

> *In order for learners to develop heuristic, or goal-directed, strategies, they must have clear goals . . . It is important to take into account the interaction between the different instructional goals, settings, techniques, and materials with which the learner is involved. More important, school districts need to coordinate remedial and classroom instruction. When reading instruction in the regular and remedial settings is different, instruction in one setting subverts instruction in the other by making it difficult for readers to apply newly learned skills.* (474–475)

It was this initial learning that shaped our belief that each student deserves a plan tailored to his or her needs. Call it an intervention or one-on-one conferring or small-group work, to us the goal is always the same: we are meeting each student's needs with tailored instruction. No longer is just "getting through the book" or the lesson our goal. It is intense, explicit teaching and scaffolded support with the students, developing them as strategic readers no matter what text they pick up.

Planning this in-class work with students takes on a life of its own. How do you manage all the paperwork, know what lesson to teach them next in small groups and individually, and what to do then? Our book *The Daily Five* helped us answer what to do with the rest of the class as we work with small groups of students or one student. We did have to figure out where the time would come from in our day to meet with all of our students. At the schools where we work, our class sizes range from twenty-four to thirty-four students. We grappled with the concept of instructional fairness. Does each student receive the exact same amount of our instructional time? Do some students need more or less, and is that fair? We agree with Richard Allington's recent research regarding instructional fairness:

> *Some teachers, the less effective ones, thought that fair meant distributing instruction equally to all students regardless of their needs. The exemplary teachers we studied, however, thought fair meant working in ways that evened out differences between students. Early in the year the exemplary teachers largely followed research by offering greater amounts of instructional time with the poorest readers in their rooms. Gradually the teachers reduced the amount of attention as those children developed better reading skills.* (2009b, 11)

To balance this out, Connor found no negative impact "for assigning the best readers more student-directed work" (2007). So, the saying "Fair is not always equal" holds true for our work with students. We no longer had to fret about meeting with each and every child one-on-one each day. There are not enough hours in the day anyway—but those realities never come into play when we are worrying; we always think we should do more.

Building the CAFE system and assessing and managing our instruction took years to try out, research, and perfect. It is a work in progress as we continue to reflect on what is working and go to the research for best practices to incorporate and refine our instruction, coaching, and support for our students.

We Are Works in Progress . . . and So Is CAFE Assessment

The CAFE system continues to evolve as we learn more about students, literacy, and what it means to be strategic, independent, thoughtful readers. But it's at a point now where we're happy to share it with you in this book.

We wrote our first book three years ago, on the Daily Five, our system for helping students do meaningful, independent work. At that time, we'd been teachers for more than fifty years collectively. We'd never written anything professionally, and we had modest expectations that anyone would read the book. About the same time, we launched a website to connect with readers of the book and others who attended our presentations.

We had no idea how these two acts—publishing a book and launching a website—would change our lives forever. During the past two years, literally thousands of the book's readers have contacted us with queries through our website and chatted with us at presentations we've done all over the country and the world. It's been really gratifying to answer these questions, and humbling to realize at times that our most honest response is "We don't know. We've never considered that."

Because we live in an Internet age, there are also discussion groups on the Web that have sprung up among teachers who have tried the Daily Five and are testing out the CAFE Assessment system in their classrooms. We can't begin to convey what a weird feeling it is for us to voyeuristically visit these discussions on occasion.

A couple of common threads appear in our conversations with colleagues throughout the country, and in their conversations with one another:

- Teachers are conscientious and want to do things "right" and well. They desire a scaffold that will support them in this endeavor.
- Teachers are offended when they are handed a script and told, "This is the way it is done—no deviations." They want freedom to adjust the scaffold to meet the diverse needs of the students they work with every day.

Our goal in writing this book is to meet both of these needs. But this isn't a scripted program, and the truth is that it will never be a finished, final product. We don't see ourselves as creators of, or salespeople for, a program—we are teachers. That is what we do every day, and it is what we do best. As we work with kids each day, we are always seeing ways to improve or refine CAFE. When you write to us or share your tweaks on message boards, inevitably we find that some of you have improved the program yourselves.

This is all a long way of saying that the materials you find in this book may be slightly different from those you received at a presentation we did two years ago, or those you will find on our website (www.thedailycafe.com) a year from now. And it's our greatest hope that our own muddling through as teachers who are always changing based on new information gives you the permission you need to keep refining and changing these materials to suit the needs of your students and your classroom schedule.

We hope you learn as much about your students and what they are capable of as readers as we do every day. And we hope you will share ways you go beyond our guidelines, to create an even stronger assessment program. And now, welcome to our CAFE!

Chapter 2

The CAFE Notebook and Record-Keeping Forms

We have tried as many different methods for keeping anecdotal notes as we have had shoes in our closets. With each new year we used to roll out a new and improved product, notebook, pen, or sticky-note extravaganza.

Our first system for keeping notes used the small 1.5-inch sticky notes. Sticky notes were relatively new and came in an assortment of pastel colors. We love office supplies, so this seemed a perfect match for our new challenge of keeping anecdotal notes. What would we write? We had no idea, really, but first things first: we would get some new tools.

We divided notebook paper into a grid, with each section large enough for the sticky notes to fit. We wrote a student's name at the top of each box. We took these pages and put them on a clipboard, and we were ready to write our notes.

With great anticipation, we began the first day of note taking. As we toured the room, we jotted on the clipboard what we noticed. Micha was reading, Natasha was reading *The Kid in the Red Jacket*, and Bella was not reading. But we then had to face the dirty little secret: we loved these little notes because we didn't really know what to write. Because they were small, we couldn't fit anything else on the paper except a note about who was reading and what they were reading—so maybe that was enough. As we went from student to student, Joan was trying to keep track of subjects by using different-colored sticky notes for each one, and Gail was having a difficult time keeping track of just where her sticky notes were.

This was our first attempt at anecdotal notes many years ago.

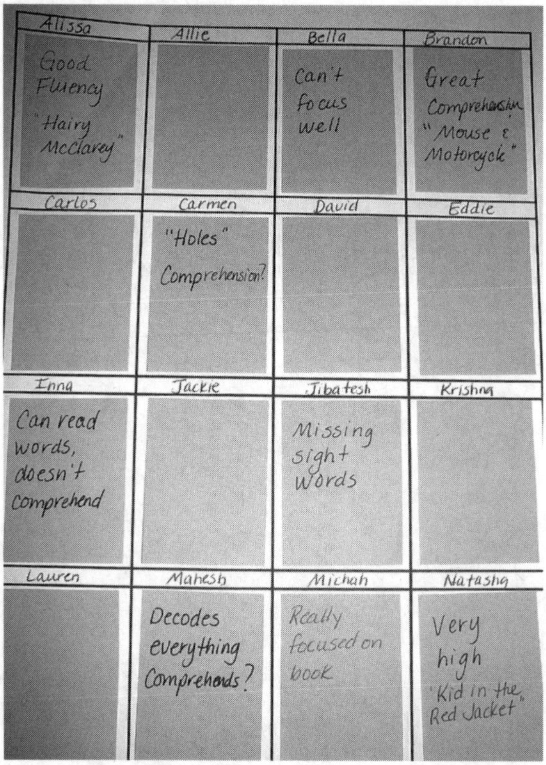

As the days and weeks wore on, Joan gave up on her color coding because she couldn't remember which color represented which subject. She was writing so many notes, the accumulating piles for each student grew to the point that the sticky notes started losing their stickiness and she found them on the floor, on her shoes, on her desk. . . . They were everywhere but on the clipboard page, with no way to trace who they belonged to.

Gail was having problems of her own. She spent her time searching for the elusive sticky-note pads. Like Hansel and Gretel, she left a trail of them wherever she went: at her desk, on the counter, or at a child's desk. Frustration led to inspiration. Decorative pins were popular at the time, and Joan and Gail often made them as craft projects on the weekends. Gail found a piece of clip art on the computer that was in the shape of a rectangle, just a bit bigger than a sticky note. She made a copy of the picture, laminated it, and hot-glued a pin on the back. After adding a stack of stickies to the front, she pinned it to her chest and—voila!—she had invented a "forever-close-at-hand" sticky-note holder.

Gail was positively giddy about her invention as she entered school the next morning. Janet—a new teacher, and one of the kindest people you could ever meet—was standing about thirty feet down the hallway. Janet never raised her voice or had an unpleasant word for anyone. As Gail walked closer to her, she held her chest out so Janet would be sure to see her new jewelry. Gail smiled in anticipation of Janet's glowing accolades for this amazing invention. Janet's mouth dropped open, and she finally blurted out, "What the @#%^@ do you have on your shirt?"

Gail was shocked—she had never heard Janet use such a forceful tone or such strong language. She quickly thought, "If she feels that strongly about my pin, it must not be the artistic statement I was thinking it was." Gail stammered a bit and said aloud, "Oh, this thing . . . my sister gave it to me. She thought I might like to use it with my sticky notes, but now that I've worn it once so I won't hurt her feelings, I can take it off."

Gail quickly walked into her classroom, unpinned the stupid pin, and threw it into her desk. Our euphoria over sticky notes had been extinguished, and we knew we had to come up with a better way to keep track of our notes.

From Notes to a Conferring Notebook: The Pensieve

After sticky notes and clipboards, we quickly moved to a notebook with pockets and different sections to hold all our anecdotal records. We have gone through many, many different styles and formats for these forms, always trying to reduce what we collect to the information we truly need to assist students and capture how they are changing and growing as readers and writers. We called this work in progress our Conferring Notebook, but even the name of the notebook has changed in recent years.

Some time ago, when we were first developing our Conferring Notebook, we were teaching classes on Thursday evenings. We often took along our notebook to share with participants.

The morning after one such class found Joan racing into school to drop off her things in the classroom, then scooting into the library in time for the early morning staff meeting, then going straight back to her room to start the day. Friday morning staff meetings always left her feeling a bit frazzled. Coupled with dropping her things in a jumbled mess in her room on the way to the meetings, this was not a calm and peaceful start to the day.

On this particular Friday, reading workshop was under way when she went to reach for her Conferring Notebook. Already frustrated by the Friday morning kerfuffle, she searched for the notebook instead of meeting with her first small strategy group. As she frantically rummaged around, she asked a couple of girls if they had seen the notebook. "My sister always calls my notebook my brain because I just can't seem to think without it," she told them. At that point, one of the students, Jacinta, turned to Joan and said, "Well, isn't your sister rude! It's not your notebook, it's your Pensieve."

Now, Jacinta was one of the very smartest students Joan has ever had the joy of teaching. The most important lesson she learned from Jacinta was always to stop and say, "Tell me more." Jacinta explained that the notebook was just like Dumbledore's Pensieve in the Harry Potter books. Jacinta was a huge Harry Potter fan and remembered minute trivia in great detail.

Jacinta explained that Dumbledore has a vessel that holds a silvery liquid. He uses his wand to take his most important thinking and memories out of his brain. In order to remember them—and to keep them where they can safely be retrieved at a later date—he transfers these ideas to the liquid in the vessel, called his Pensieve. "The notebook is really your Pensieve," she said, "because you always write in it your most important thinking about us!" As Joan stared at Jacinta with her mouth open, she couldn't help but be impressed by Jacinta's profound understanding of Dumbledore's Pensieve and the important role it plays in his life. This is just like the vital role the Conferring Notebook plays in our lives: we use it to hold assessment data, daily observations, and our teaching and learning. Joan couldn't wait to tell Gail, and the term *Pensieve* has stuck ever since.

Although the new name remained, the simple white notebook did not. We realized that one reason we were always losing our Pensieves was that they looked so much like all the other notebooks in our rooms. Now, each summer, as soon as school supplies appear in the stores, we begin the search for the most beautiful notebook we can find. When we locate the perfect

Janet loves her Conferring Notebook.

notebook, we usually purchase two, because we use them so much that they often fall apart midyear. Having notebooks that reflect our personalities also has its advantages: if we set the Pensieves down somewhere—in the workroom, staff room, or bathroom—others recognize whose they are and return them to us. When we introduce the notebook to teachers, we're often surprised at how important it is to them to personalize it, to pick one with a color scheme, look, and feel that they love. We're going to take you through how we set up our Pensieves, because once you set yours up, you'll have a better sense of how these records are an integral part of the CAFE system.

We have helped thousands of teachers implement CAFE in their schools, and we've found that the best place to begin is often with a "notebook party." We bring in blank notebooks, templates, dividers, and copies of the forms everyone will need. Teachers love to personalize this material. In fact, some reject the plain notebooks supplied by their districts and come up with lovely materials that reflect their own personal styles.

We shouldn't be surprised. The CAFE notebook is something you'll carry with you all the time during literacy workshops. Your students will come to recognize it, and like a writer's notebook, it should be something that feels comfortable and right for you in terms of size and style.

We spent many years developing our CAFE notebook—testing it out, refining elements that were useful, and discarding those that weren't. We're always refining it, but right now our Pensieves include the following sections and components. We've provided templates in the appendix for each form listed here.

Section 1 of the Pensieve: Teacher Notes

The first section of the book is for organizing and planning our time with the entire class. This is where we note when we will confer with individual students and small groups, and where we track how often we've met with everyone.

Figure 2.1 Joan's calendar

January

Sunday	Monday	Tuesday	Wednesday	Thursday	Friday	Saturday
	1	2 Amanda	3 Juan Katie Mahesh	4 Ikman Haley	5 Juan Katie Mahesh	6
7	8 Sevilya Inna	9 Sevilya Inna Haley	10 Sevilya Inna	11 Sevilya Inna	12 Inna Jaeger	13
14	15 Inna Jaeger	16 Colin Carlos	17 Inna Josh	18 Julia Devon	19 Mahesh Nadjae	20
21	22 Colin Josh Devon Nadjae	23 Sandy Simon	24 Sevilya Devon Zach	25 Sandy Samuel Brandon	26 Sevilya Simon Brandon	27
28	29 Colin Devon	30 Donita Zach	31 Donita			

Calendar

We use the calendar (Figure 2.1) to make appointments with each child. After conferring with a child, we might end the meeting with, "Since today is Tuesday, and you'll need at least tomorrow's workshop to work on your fluency goal, we'll plan to meet Thursday" or "Today is Monday, and it sounds like we'll need to meet again tomorrow about this, so let's schedule a conference for Tuesday." The calendar is crucial for keeping track of the commitments we've made to individual children, and for making sure we aren't overcommitted throughout the week. (Please see Chapter 4, "Conferring with Children," for more information on conferring procedures.)

It raises accountability for teachers and students in ways that are almost immeasurable. If Brandon is reading a book in the Magic Treehouse series, we might say, "You've read two chapters since yesterday, and we need to meet by the time you've finished Chapter 8. At your current pace, that means we need to meet in three days. Or do you think you might complete the chapters more quickly?" The calendar is also very useful for students who want continual attention. We can say, "Remember, we're meeting on Thursday about your goal. Today is only Tuesday."

We are more focused on what will be accomplished day by day in reading workshops between our conferences when we and the student commit to a date on the calendar. As many researchers note, kids need to read voraciously, and the calendar can be a gentle nudge toward completing more reading for some children (Allington 2009a, 2009b; Cunningham 2009; Kuhn et al. 2006; McGill-Franzen and Allington 2008).

We also use the calendar to note the strategy-group meetings, and when we next have to meet with any group. These groups are flexible and always shifting in terms of who is in which one and what the goal is, so the calendar is helpful for remembering the group commitments.

Keeping Track Form

This is a simple grid with each child's name on it and the date of our conference so that we have a record of when we have met with each child (Figure 2.2). Our goal is not to meet with each child an equal number of times. Depending on the child, where he or she is in development as a reader or writer, and his or her specific needs, we may meet twice a day, once a day, or only once or twice in a given week.

What's important to us is that each child's needs are met. For some children, it's a mark of their growing strengths as readers and sophistication that they require fewer individual conferences with us. They may have goals that call for more sustained time in books and may have developed the stamina to go for longer periods without support from us. But the form is also a check for us if we have missed a child who needs support—it ensures that no one slips through the cracks.

Figure 2.2 Sample Keeping Track form

Keeping Track: Reading Writing

Amanda	11/2	11/5	11/10	11/15	11/16	11/19	11/24	11/26	11/31															
Brandon	11/2	11/4	11/8	11/9	11/16	11/19	11/24	11/29	11/31															
Carlos	11/2	11/4	11/9	11/10	11/16	11/19	11/25	11/29	11/31															
Colin	11/2	11/4	11/8	11/10	11/16	11/22	11/25	11/29	11/31															
Devon	11/2	11/8	11/12	11/18	11/22	11/27	11/31																	
Donita	11/12	11/18	11/25																					
Haley	11/2	11/9	11/10	11/16	11/19	11/25	11/30																	
Ikman	11/4	11/11	11/18	11/25																				
Inna	11/8	11/9	11/10	11/11	11/15	11/17	11/19	11/26	11/31															
Jaeger	11/12	11/15	11/22	11/29																				
Josh	11/9	11/16	11/23	11/30																				
Juan	11/3	11/10	11/17	11/24	11/31																			
Julia	11/4	11/12	11/18	11/26																				
Katie	11/3	11/5	11/8	11/12	11/17	11/23	11/24	11/30	11/31															
Mahesh	11/3	11/5	11/8	11/12	11/18	11/23	11/24	11/30																
Nadjae	11/5	11/8	11/11	11/12	11/15	11/17	11/19	11/22	11/24	11/26	11/30													
Samuel	11/3	11/5	11/9	11/15	11/18	11/23	11/25	11/30																
Sandy	11/3	11/8	11/9	11/15	11/17	11/23	11/25	11/30																
Sevilya	11/8	11/9	11/10	11/11	11/18	11/24	11/26	11/30																
Simon	11/3	11/8	11/9	11/15	11/17	11/24	11/26	11/30																
Zach	11/3	11/8	11/9	11/15	11/17	11/23	11/25	11/29	11/30	11/31														

Strategy Groups Form

We use the Strategy Groups form (Figure 2.3) to create flexible groups based on similar goals among children. These are not ability groups. Often a group working on something like fluency will include children reading at a wide range of different levels, in different books. As clusters of children emerge with the same goals, we note this on this form.

Figure 2.3 Sample Strategy Groups form

Strategy Groups and Instruction

Goal Fluency	Strategy Reread Text	Names	Touch Points
Date	**Lesson**		
1-17	Model—Shel Silverstein poem—Practice as a group	Katie	3
1-19	Review poem—Review strategy—practice		
1-23	Check group for good-fit books—students share reading their own stories.	Colin	4
1-25	Bring in poetry books, each choose and practice	Zach	3, 3
1-29	Partner Read and practice		
1-31	Most are getting this—make sure they have good-fit books	Josh	4, 4, 4
2-2	Students state their purpose for using this strategy		

Goal Accuracy	Strategy Use Beginning and Ending Sounds	Names	Touch Points
Date	**Lesson**		
1-15	Use Jack and Jill Nursery Rhyme—recite rhyme together—frame the word j-a-c-k. Look at beginning and ending sounds, do the same with Jill.	Nadjae Haley	
1-16	Review beginning and ending sounds. Review Jack & Jill. Point and choose <u>hill</u> to frame and stretch each sound. Use leveled books with 1 sentence on each page—read and frame.	Colin	
1-17	Use Humpty Dumpty—recite poem—frame 2 words read together focusing on beginning and ending sounds. Review books from yesterday. Choral read. Choose 2 words to focus on beg. and end.	Donita	

Goal Vocabulary	Strategy Tune In to Interesting Words 2/7 add—Use prior knowledge . . .	Names	Touch Points
Date	**Lesson**		
1-10	Introduce word collectors—purpose—how to use Add 2 words a day from their reading	Brandon	
1-17	Review word collectors—what do your words mean—how do you figure out the meaning	Ikman	
1-24	May need to add Use prior knowledge and context to predict and confirm meaning—review each word collector	Samuel	
2-7	Started layering on Use prior knowledge	Sandy	

At the completion of each individual assessment, we turn to the Strategy Groups form and check to see whether any other students we have already assessed need support with the same strategy as the child with whom we are working. If so, we pop the child's name into the box on the form along with others. If we find no one with that need yet, we begin a new box and wait to see if anyone else will emerge to add to the group.

Figure 2.3 Sample Strategy Groups form *(continued)*

Strategy Groups and Instruction

Goal Comprehension **Strategy** Check for Understanding		**Names**	**Touch Points**
Date	**Lesson**		
1-10	Bring read-aloud to group—Model from today's readings, all practice	Sevilya	
1-11	Each practice in own book	Inna	3
1-12	I will call on each one during read-aloud to practice—How did it go?	Sandy	3, 4, 4
1-16	When do you use this strategy? Each share with group—give examples in own story	Juan	3
1-18	Partner group—practice with own stories with other person checking for understanding		

Goal Accuracy **Strategy** Flip the Sounds		**Names**	**Touch Points**
Date	**Lesson**		
1-10	Whiteboard—Review long and short "a"—practice flipping	Jaeger	
1-11	Whiteboard—Review flipping sounds with "a"		
1-12	Whiteboard—Review long and short "i"—flip "i" and "a" words	Amanda	4, 4, 4
1-15	Whiteboard—Review "a" and "i" sounds find in own books		
1-16	Whiteboard—Review "o" sounds—flip each	Josh	
1-17	Whiteboard—Review a, i, o—flip and find in own books		
1-18	" —Review "e" sounds—flip each—practice	Haley	
1-19	" —Review a, e, i, o flip and find in books		
		Colin	3, 4

Goal Comprehension **Strategy** Summarize Text; Include Sequence of Main Events		**Names**	**Touch Points**
Date	**Lesson**		
1-12	Define summary—model one verbally using the class read-aloud	Devon	
1-18	Sandy joined—review summarize, students share their own interpretation. I write in front of the group a summary from our read-aloud. Adding critical elements.	Brandon	
		Simon	
1-24	Partnered—each child tells the other a summary of their own book so far—in 4–5 sentences. Listen for main elements—Repeat back. Student writes summary from their own story—bring it back next time.	Sandy	

Once a group or individuals show they have mastered the strategy and are ready for a new goal, we cross their names off the sheet. It's messy at times, but effective. (Please see Chapter 5, "Eavesdropping on Some Conferences," for more information on small-group procedures.)

Section 2 of the Pensieve: Dividers/Tabs for Each Child

Each child has his or her own section of the notebook so that we can easily flip to that child's name when we meet with him or her in conferences or record notes after a small-group session.

Within each child's section, there is a

- CAFE Menu (Figure 2.4),
- Reading Conference form (Figure 2.5), and
- Writing Conference form (in the appendix)

At the top of each form, there is space to note the child's current strengths and goals. The forms include a space for us to record instruction we've provided to help the child meet the goal (individually, in a small group, or with the whole class) and what we've observed with the child related to the goal. There is also a space to record what steps the child will take with our assistance to meet his or her goal. As the child meets the goals and the page is filled, we add additional sheets to his or her section in the book.

Each student has a divider page of his or her own in our Pensieve.

The Literacy CAFE Menu

Comprehension I understand what I read	**Accuracy** I can read the words	**Fluency** I can read accurately, with expression, and understand what I read	**Expand Vocabulary** I know, find, and use interesting words
Strategies Check for understanding Back up and reread Monitor and fix up Retell the story Use prior knowledge to connect with text Make a picture or mental image Ask questions throughout the reading process Predict what will happen; use text to confirm Infer and support with evidence Use text features (titles, headings, captions, graphic features) Summarize text; include sequence of main events Use main idea and supporting details to determine importance Determine and analyze author's purpose and support with text Recognize literacy elements (genre, plot, character, setting, problem/resolution, theme) Recognize and explain cause-and-effect relationships Compare and contrast within and between text	***Strategies*** Cross checking . . . Do the pictures and/or words look right? Do they sound right? Do they make sense? Use the pictures . . . Do the words and pictures match? Use beginning and ending sounds Blend sounds; stretch and reread Flip the sound Chunk letters and sounds together Skip the word, then come back Trade a word/guess a word that makes sense	***Strategies*** Voracious reading Read appropriate-level texts that are a good fit Reread text Practice common sight words and high-frequency words Adjust and apply different reading rates to match text Use punctuation to enhance phrasing and prosody (end marks, commas, etc.)	***Strategies*** Voracious reading Tune in to interesting words and use new vocabulary in speaking and writing Use pictures, illustrations, and diagrams Use word parts to determine the meaning of words (prefixes, suffixes, origins, abbreviations, etc.) Use prior knowledge and context to predict and confirm meaning Ask someone to define the word for you Use dictionaries, thesauruses, and glossaries as tools

Behaviors That Support Reading

Get started right away Stay in one place Work quietly Read the whole time Increase stamina Select and read good-fit books

Figure 2.4 CAFE Menu

We prefer the simplicity of these forms to the more complicated developmental checklists or the set conferring questions we've used in the past. We haven't found a checklist yet that captures the diverse abilities of children, so invariably the checklist ends up blank for a few children and fully completed for a few others too quickly.

We often make minor changes and adjustments to these forms, as do the teachers who use them. But it's really a very simple system for keeping anecdotal records, as you'll see when we move into examples of using the notebook in conferences with students during the first days and weeks of school.

Figure 2.5 Joan's Reading Conference form

Reading Conference

Strengths Accuracy and Fluency **Student** Inna

Goals and Strategies Comprehension Check for Understanding

Date Touch Point	Observation and Instruction	Next Steps to Meet Goal
Date 1-8 **Touch Point**	Amber Brown Is Not a Crayon Sounds beautiful—No comprehension Teach—Model Check for Understanding	1. Think while reading 2. Stop at ends of paragraphs 3. Practice "I just read . . . Who, what Meet tomorrow
Date 1-9 **Touch Point**	Amber Brown · Stopped at end of paragraph Who Amber What . . . · Couldn't answer! · Went back to sentence level and reviewed who, what.	1. Stop and think while reading 2. Who . . . what . . . at end of each paragraph Meet tomorrow
Date 1-10 **Touch Point**	Amber Brown Difficult to remember Brought picture book The Incredible Adventures to help support meaning.	1. Read picture book 2. Read to Someone and practice ✓ for Understanding Tomorrow
Date 1-11 3 **Touch Point**	Reread Incredible Adventures . . . was able to ✓ for understanding at end of page Partner reading is helping Keep this up!	1. Read another picture book 2. Read to Someone, ✓ for Understanding Meet tomorrow
Date 1-12 3 **Touch Point**	Read Amber Brown 2nd day she is getting it even with chapter book Practice	1. Read Amber Brown 2. Read to Someone and ✓ for Understanding Meet every other day
Date 1-15 3 **Touch Point**	Amber Brown Able to ✓ for Under. by paragraph She said Read to Someone is helpful.	1. Amber Brown 2. Read to Someone 3. Sticky note 4. Begin writing in journal 2 examples of ✓ for Understanding Meet 2 day

Chapter 3

CAFE Step-by-Step: The First Days of School

We both love a good recipe. When someone cooks or bakes something we like, we ask for the recipe—and then when it's given to us, we ask for even more advice. Are there any special tips we should know for baking in our wet Seattle climate? Are there any ways the veteran chef has changed the recipe to make it even tastier?

We get as much advice as we can, in as much detail as possible, when we are first trying any new recipe. It's a funny thing, though: we want as many details as possible for how to make the recipe work well so that we can then turn around and eventually make our own adjustments to it.

Before teachers are ready to fine-tune the use of CAFE Assessment in their own classrooms, the bulk of their questions are about how to launch the program in the first days and weeks of school. Since the launching charts for the Daily Five in our first book remain the most popular component of that book, we've included similar launching charts for CAFE in the appendix. In this chapter, we want to give you our recipe for success during those crucial first few days and weeks of school. We have tried to be very detailed in our description, down to the language we use with students. We don't expect you to use the same language or even follow the order of lessons, but you're more likely to find your own recipe for success if we're clear about what we do and why we do it.

The CAFE Menu bulletin board is empty when school starts, waiting for group learning to be posted.

Preparation for CAFE can begin before school even starts, or it may begin at some point during the school year. It gets under way when we put up the bulletin board. It has to be in a space low enough for children to access it, and it has to be large enough to be added to as the school year progresses. The dimensions of the board in Joan's room last year were 5 feet by 5 feet.

Throughout this book, we share demonstration lessons and examples of individual conferring about dozens of strategies that fall under CAFE. It's important to realize that we don't introduce all these strategies to students at the start of the year (or whenever we begin using CAFE). In fact, with primary students, we are most likely by the end of the year to have introduced the CAFE strategies highlighted in Figure 3.1. Intermediate students or more

The Literacy CAFE Menu

Comprehension I understand what I read	**Accuracy** I can read the words	**Fluency** I can read accurately, with expression, and understand what I read	**Expand Vocabulary** I know, find, and use interesting words
Strategies	***Strategies***	***Strategies***	***Strategies***
Check for understanding	Cross checking . . . Do the pictures and/or words look right? Do they sound right? Do they make sense?	Voracious reading	Voracious reading
Back up and reread	Use the pictures . . . Do the words and pictures match?	Read appropriate-level texts that are a good fit	Tune in to interesting words and use new vocabulary in speaking and writing
Monitor and fix up	Use beginning and ending sounds	Reread text	Use pictures, illustrations, and diagrams
Retell the story	Blend sounds; stretch and reread	Practice common sight words and high-frequency words	Use word parts to determine the meaning of words (prefixes, suffixes, origins, abbreviations, etc.)
Use prior knowledge to connect with text	Flip the sound	Adjust and apply different reading rates to match text	Use prior knowledge and context to predict and confirm meaning
Make a picture or mental image	Chunk letters and sounds together	Use punctuation to enhance phrasing and prosody (end marks, commas, etc.)	Ask someone to define the word for you
Ask questions throughout the reading process	Skip the word, then come back		Use dictionaries, thesauruses, and glossaries as tools
Predict what will happen; use text to confirm	Trade a word/guess a word that makes sense		
Infer and support with evidence			
Use text features (titles, headings, captions, graphic features)			
Summarize text; include sequence of main events			
Use main idea and supporting details to determine importance			
Determine and analyze author's purpose and support with text			
Recognize literacy elements (genre, plot, character, setting, problem/resolution, theme)			
Recognize and explain cause-and-effect relationships			
Compare and contrast within and between text			

Behaviors That Support Reading

Get started right away Stay in one place Work quietly Read the whole time Increase stamina Select and read good-fit books

Figure 3.1
Highlighted CAFE Menu

advanced primary classrooms will likely have all the strategies introduced by the end of the year.

But at the start of the year, there are no strategies on the board. When students enter our classroom on the first day of school, they see the board with its bright colors and CAFE headings.

Each heading has a brief definition under it:

Comprehension: "I understand what I read"
Accuracy: "I can read the words"
Fluency: "I can read accurately, with expression, and understand what I read"
Expand Vocabulary: "I know, find, and use interesting words"

Underneath each heading is a blank rectangular sheet of paper awaiting students' handwritten names on sticky notes. These serve as a visual

CAFE bulletin board headings are followed by definitions.

reminder of their goals as we settle into workshop routines. Below the blank rectangular sheet for goals is another, larger blank area that students will fill collaboratively throughout the year as we teach and they master new skills and strategies under each of the four headings. Next to the board is a small holder with blank multicolored, lined cards (3 by 9 inches), which we have ready for writing out each strategy and adding to the board throughout the year.

These strategy cards were filled out by students, with blank cards, on the left, ready for more strategies.

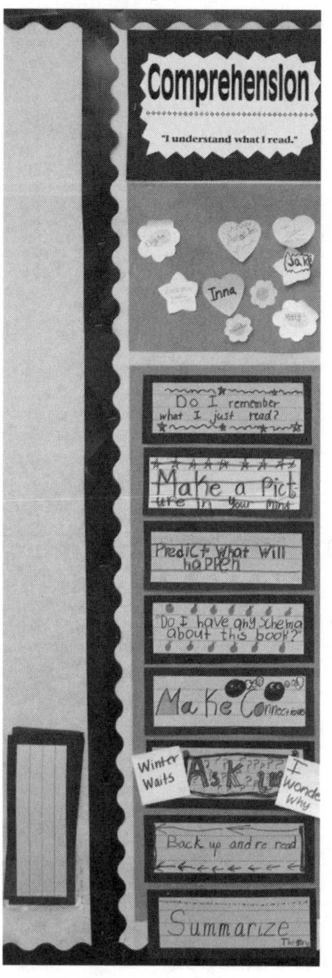

First Day: First Read-Aloud; Whole-Group Strategy Lesson One

On the first day of school, after greetings, we bring students together on the floor for our first read-aloud and lesson.

We don't talk about the CAFE board, and there is already so much that is new for children to explore and discover in the classroom that few of them notice or say anything about it. For students who have never been exposed to CAFE, we begin with a read-aloud of a picture book to teach the first strategy, Check for Understanding. This is always the first strategy we teach to all grade levels, because everything we do in reading is anchored to comprehension and monitoring the making of meaning while reading.

We launch the lesson with these words: "Girls and boys, as I read aloud to you today, I'm going to model how readers use a very important comprehension strategy, called Check for Understanding. Every book is written because the author has something they want to tell us. Sometimes it is to understand something or learn something new, or it may be to tell us a story. The secret to this strategy is remembering to think about what the author is telling us when we read and to stop often to check for understanding, which means we want to be sure we are understanding what we read."

Great First-Day Read-Alouds for Teaching Introductory Strategies

The great thing about books with short and fairly simple text is that they really help us keep our focus lesson concise. We want the text, though brief, to be a great read-aloud that captures the interest of our youngest learners. These titles often meet that need.

Title	Author
Ape in a Cape; An Alphabet of Odd Animals	Fritz Eichenberg
Bark George	Jules Feiffer
Don't Let the Pigeon Drive the Bus	Mo Willems
Good Night, Gorilla	Peggy Rathmann
How to Be	Lisa Brown
I'm the Biggest Thing in the Ocean	Kevin Sherry
Kitten's First Full Moon	Kevin Henkes
Monkey and Me	Emily Gravett
My Friend Is Sad	Mo Willems
No, David	David Shannon
The OK Book	Amy Drouse Rosenthal
Tomorrow's Alphabet	George Shannon
What Will Fat Cat Sit On?	Jan Thomas

Picture books are a great source for modeling strategies, and we use them with all students, both primary and intermediate. Any titles in your own classroom library would work for CAFE lessons. The following are some of our favorites.

Title	Author
An Egg Is Quiet	Dianna Aston
Bad Kitty	Nick Bruel
Beatrice Doesn't Want To	Laura Numeroff
Bertie Was a Watchdog	Rick Walton
Bippity Bop Barbershop	Natasha Anastasia Tarpley
Chester	Melanie Watt
Cook-A-Doodle-Doo!	Janet Stevens and Susan Stevens Crummell
Duck & Goose	Tad Hills
Elizabeti's Doll	Stephanie Stuve Bodeen
Four Feet, Two Sandals	Karen Lynn Williams

Fox in Love	Edward Marshall
Froggy Gets Dressed	Jonathan London
The Garden of Abdul Gasazi	Chris Van Allsburg
How I Became a Pirate	Melinda Long
I Wanna Iguana	Karen Kaufman Orloff
Ish	Peter Reynolds
Knuffle Bunny: A Cautionary Tale	Mo Willems
Leonardo, the Terrible Monster	Mo Willems
Love and Roast Chicken: A Trickster Tale from the Andes Mountains	Barbara Knutson
Mary Smith	Andrea U'Ren
Mr. Peabody's Apples **	Madonna and Loren Long
Mudball	Matt Tavares
Music for Alice **	Allen Say
My Dog Is as Smelly as Dirty Socks; and Other Funny Family Portraits	Hanoch Piven
My Lucky Day	Keiko Kasza
My Name Is Yoon	Helen Recorvits and Gabi Swiatkowska
Once upon a Cool Motorcycle Dude	Kevin O'Malley, Carol Heyer, and Scott Goto
Piper	Emma Chichester Clark
Precious and the Boo Hag	Patricia C. McKissack and Onawumi Jean Moss
Superhero ABC	Bob McLeod
Taking a Bath with the Dog and Other Things That Make Me Happy	Scott Menchin
Tops & Bottoms	Janet Stevens
What Do You Do with a Tail Like This?	Robin Page and Steve Jenkins

***Content and/or length makes it more suitable for intermediate students.*

With every age group, we try to read aloud at least one picture book and a portion of an ongoing chapter book each day. These books provide the perfect venue for introducing and modeling strategies with both shorter and longer texts.

We select a picture book with five to eight lines of text on each page, beautiful illustrations, and a great story line. After reading a page or two, we stop and tell the students, "Before I go any further, I need to use my comprehension strategy and stop and check for understanding. I don't want to keep reading if I don't know what is going on in the story." When we model Check for Understanding, we stop every few pages and talk aloud, explaining the sense we are making of the text. Other times we model that we can't remember what we read, or that it doesn't make sense. We believe it is just as important to model what we do when our understanding breaks down.

"Boys and girls, did you notice that when I stopped to check for understanding, I didn't understand what was happening in the story? I can't continue to keep reading if I don't know what the author was just trying to tell me or I won't understand the rest of the story. So when I don't understand what I am reading, here is what I do: I back up and reread." We continue with this type of modeling through the whole book.

At the end of the book, we pull out a blank strategy card from the holder next to the CAFE board. "Boys and girls, I just modeled for you one of the most important strategies readers use. Does anyone remember what words I used to describe this strategy?" Students call out "Check for Understanding," or we share the words with them. We write the words on the strategy card in front of the students, and post them under Comprehension. This is the first strategy we post every year, because it is the most important one for most readers.

We then introduce the CAFE Menu board to them. "This is the board we'll use all year to remind you of the reading strategies that all readers use. We put strategies up on this board so that you can look at and try many different strategies as you read. It's a menu. How many of you have ever been to a restaurant? They hand you a menu, or you look up above the counter to see all the choices of the things you can eat."

Most students have experience with menus, even if it's just from a fast-food restaurant. We explain, "When you're picking out food from a restaurant menu, you make choices depending on what sounds tasty to eat, and what will be healthy for you. When you are reading, you choose different strategies to understand different types of books. If you're reading your favorite picture book, you might use certain strategies. If you're reading magazines or newspapers, you might have other ways of making sense of what you're reading. If you're reading on the Internet or gathering information on the computer, other strategies might be more effective."

Depending on the age of the students, we adjust our language to the kinds of texts they are most likely to see and use daily.

At this point, we've introduced only one comprehension strategy. That is plenty for the first book we've read aloud and for the lesson to introduce CAFE. We will reinforce and refer to this Check for Understanding strategy repeatedly through the first days and weeks of school. We do not introduce or explain the other headings on the board at this time—it would be too much for students to observe, and they wouldn't have any concrete experiences of watching us model or discussing a book linked to the heading to anchor their learning.

The first days of school are a challenge, no matter the age of the students. After a summer at home, few have the stamina for extended reading and writing on their own. Many routines need to be introduced. After all these years, we still find the first day of school a little overwhelming, too! Because of this, we often read three or four picture books the first day of school to ease students into routines and build community. These first-day read-alouds are the perfect opportunity to reinforce Check for Understanding, as well as to introduce a couple more strategies to add to the board. We even physically touch the Check for Understanding card as we mention the strategy again on the first day, or during the first weeks of school, so it becomes anchored in the students' minds.

First Day: Second Read-Aloud; Whole-Group Strategy Lesson Two

After this first read-aloud, we move into establishing the Daily Five routines for independent work in our classroom. If you aren't using Daily Five, this is probably when you will introduce other routines and expectations for students. After students have had some time to work independently (however briefly) and explore the room a bit, we bring them back for another read-aloud and explanation of a second strategy.

This second strategy will go under a different heading on the board, so we choose something that fits under Accuracy, Fluency, or Expand Vocabulary. Which strategy you choose to introduce depends on the group of students and their needs. However, we have found in our years of working with the CAFE Menu and its strategies that we typically introduce the same ones the first few days of school.

"Boys and girls, I have a wonderful book I am going to read to you. As I read this, I am going to model again the comprehension strategy Check for Understanding." We point again to this strategy card on the CAFE Menu. "Remember, *comprehension* means 'I understand what I read.'"

We begin reading the book aloud, once again stopping often to check for understanding, each time pointing to that strategy card on our CAFE Menu so we anchor the modeling and conversation about this strategy to the visual organizer. In previous years, we would post many beautiful displays on our walls at the start of the year, never to refer to them again. We hoped students would look at the walls and use the information as they were reading and writing—but not surprisingly, with no anchor in experience or personal background knowledge, these lovely displays were just colorful wallpaper for students that might as well have been written in Sanskrit.

We now know that students will not refer to the walls if we aren't constantly referring to them ourselves—not only pointing to or reading off the walls but actually moving our hands to the information that is needed.

We often teach Cross Checking under the Accuracy heading as the second strategy on the second day of school.

"Boys and girls, I have already modeled a strategy readers use when they are trying to comprehend, or understand, what they read. While I read this book, I will continue to show you how readers use that strategy, but I am also going to introduce you to another very important strategy that all readers use, even adults. This next strategy is used when you are trying to read the words of a book. It is called Cross Checking and fits right here under Accuracy on our CAFE Menu. *Accuracy* means 'I can read the words.'"

We begin reading the book, modeling the strategy previously introduced. At one point in the story, we will come to a word we don't know and say, "I'm not sure what this word is. I think I'll try Cross Checking. Perhaps that strategy will help me read the word." *Cross Checking* means I need to try reading the word and then ask myself three questions: 1) "Does what I just read look right; do the letters and/or pictures match what I am saying?" (We take one arm and cross it over our body so our hand is on the opposite shoulder.); 2) "Does it sound right?" (We take the other hand and cross it over our body to the opposite shoulder so that we have a cross in front of us.); and 3) "Does it make sense?" (both arms drop down to our sides).

"Let me try it out." We read the difficult word, thinking out loud as we model how to cross-check. We make the hand motions as well.

As we continue to read, we can also model this strategy by reading a word incorrectly and not stopping. Instead, we read on to the end of the

Cross Checking: "Does it look right?"

"Does it sound right?"

"Does it make sense?"

sentence, where we stop and say, "Hey, something didn't make sense. I'm going to read it again and see if I can figure out which word I missed."

We back up and read the sentence again, this time taking note of which word is causing problems. We repeat the same directions as above to help us figure out the incorrect word.

At the end of the story, we review. "Boys and girls, I just modeled again the comprehension strategy of Check for Understanding." (Point it out on the CAFE board.) "You also saw a brand new strategy under Accuracy, called Cross Checking. Remember that *accuracy* means 'I can read the words.'"

We then take out a blank strategy card, write down "Cross Checking—Do the pictures and/or words look right, sound right, and make sense?" and add it to the CAFE Menu. "Wow, we have two strategy cards up on our CAFE Menu. We'll keep using these strategies all year long."

First Day: Third Read-Aloud; Whole-Group Strategy Lesson Three

Because it's the first day and routines for independent work aren't fully in place yet, there is usually time for a third picture book at some point during the morning or afternoon. We typically introduce Tune In to Interesting Words, under the heading Expand Vocabulary next.

"Girls and boys, today I'm excited to introduce you to another one of our CAFE Menu items, Expand Vocabulary. *Expand Vocabulary* means 'to know, find, and use interesting words.' We want to learn more and more words so we can read them and know what they mean as well as use them in our reading and speaking. We are going to learn many interesting words this year. I can hardly wait! Today as I am reading this book, I am going to be watching for interesting words and really tune in to them, which means 'to pay attention to them.'"

For this strategy lesson, we choose excellent children's literature to read to students so that there are always interesting words to model tuning in to. As we read the picture book, we stop once or twice in the story, pausing to remark or comment on a word that strikes us as particularly interesting. It might sound something like this: "Did you hear the word I read? I love that word! It sounds so interesting and feels delightful as I say it. Aren't words wonderful? Tuning in to interesting words is a great strategy for expanding our vocabulary. As we grow as readers, we want to learn many new words to expand our vocabularies."

We find that our enthusiasm and excitement for finding and taking delight in interesting words is contagious. At this moment, we're not as concerned about defining the words with students as we are about getting them to tune in to interesting language. This strategy will help them pull up and pause when they don't understand an exotic word, to check for understanding. It will also help them ferret out new words they can use during writing workshop.

While we are reading this third book, we continue to model the other strategies previously introduced: Check for Understanding and Cross Checking. Each time we model these strategies, we stop, reach over, and touch the corresponding cards on the CAFE Menu board. At the completion of the read-aloud, once again we take another blank strategy card and write, "Tune in to interesting words and use new vocabulary in speaking and writing" on it. We post it under the Expand Vocabulary section of the board.

"Boys and girls, we have another strategy up on our CAFE Menu. It is so exciting! I just modeled for you the Expand Vocabulary strategy of Tune In to Interesting Words. It is a wonderful strategy for expanding your vocabulary, and all it takes is paying attention to words as you read! Today we have added three brand-new strategy cards to our CAFE Menu."

We then go back and review the three strategies added to the CAFE board, each time touching the cards as we talk about the strategies and the books we used to introduce them.

Second Day: Whole-Group Strategy Lesson One

Another strategy that we find is crucial to teach within the first day or two of school is Back Up and Reread.

"Boys and girls, I am going to teach you another comprehension strategy. It is called *Back Up and Reread.* You might already know this strategy. Let me show you how I use it when I am reading. When I was reading to you and I got to the end of this section, I used the Comprehension strategy Check for Understanding. I couldn't remember what I'd read, so now I'm going to turn back to the beginning of this section and reread it. The secret to making this strategy work is that I have to really pay attention to what I am reading. Sometimes I need to slow down and back up to read it more slowly so I can really think about the meaning." We reread the section again, this time more slowly while enunciating the words clearly.

"Class, I just reread the section. Now I will try my other strategy of Check for Understanding to see if backing up and rereading helped me understand what I read. Let's see, I just read that the friends were having lunch and were going to spend the night at Kelsey's house. Wow, Back Up and Reread helped me remember what I just read.

"Think about it: I just used two of the strategies together to help me remember my reading. I started with Check for Understanding. When I couldn't remember what I'd read, I backed up and reread the section and then checked for understanding again, and I could remember what was happening in the story."

At this time, we reach over and grab a blank strategy card and write "Back Up and Reread" on the card.

"Boys and girls, I am going to add this strategy to our CAFE Menu right here under Comprehension. When you are reading today and you don't remember what you read, try the strategy of Back Up and Reread and see if it will work for you."

Though all the strategies are important, these four are ones we will refer to over and over in whole-class, small-group, and individual-conference settings. We want them introduced within the first day or two of the school year.

With each read-aloud and whole-class lesson, we're continuing to review and model the strategies Check for Understanding, Tune In to Interesting Words, Back Up and Reread, and Cross Checking. We keep reinforcing the menu metaphor by explaining that it's just like a menu at a restaurant: you don't normally order just one thing. You might order a main course and a dessert or an appetizer and a beverage. We explain that readers do the same thing as they read. They don't use just one strategy but often try out two or three when they get confused or struggle to make sense of a text until they find the one or two that work for them.

We focus on those four strategies for at least a few days, repeating them and modeling them in our first read-alouds, constantly going back and anchoring students to the CAFE Menu board as we read. We don't want to introduce too many strategies too quickly, because as you all know, we have so many other things that need our attention in the first few days of school. Even with students who have experience with the CAFE Menu, we reteach and reinforce some of these core strategies during the first few days of school.

From Whole-Class Lessons to Individual Conferences: Assessment to Instruction

After the first few days, our room is settling into a predictable routine. As a class we are learning strategies from the CAFE Menu, the kids are starting to build stamina through Daily Five, and at the same time we begin meeting with students individually to assess their reading strengths and help them declare their goals. We call this process Assessment to Instruction (see Figure 3.2).

We use seven steps to guide us from assessing a student to knowing the type of instruction they will need.

Step 1: Assess Individual Student

When we meet one-on-one with students, we administer a running record, a Developmental Reading Assessment (DRA) or Individualized Reading

Figure 3.2
Assessment to Instruction

Assessment to Instruction

1. Assess individual student.
2. Discuss findings with student.
3. Set goal and identify strategies with student.
4. Student declares goal on menu and in notebook.
5. Teacher fills out individual Reading Conference form.
6. Teacher fills out Strategy Groups form.
7. Instruction.

Joan assesses Inna.

Inventory (IRI), check for concepts of print for emergent readers, and do a fluency check for more advanced readers.

But regardless of the assessment you use, you can look for the same things we look for. We are trying to figure out each child's strengths as a reader, and their greatest area of need.

Step 2: Discuss Findings with Student

As we assess the children individually, they already have some background knowledge of what the CAFE Menu is and why we will be using it this year. This background knowledge may come from the students' previous experiences with the CAFE Menu, or from our work the first days of school on whole-group focus lessons and starting to build the CAFE Menu board together.

After assessing a child, we begin the discussion of what we learned from the assessment with "Tell me about yourself as a reader."

Students who have never answered this question may look at you like a deer caught in the headlights. They might say, "I like to read" or "I don't like to read," and little else.

"Tell me about yourself as a reader."

At that point, we usually say, "Let me tell you what I noticed about you as a reader."

"Let me tell you what I noticed about you as a reader."

If they exhibit few skills or reading behaviors because they are very young, we can always compliment them on being good at listening to stories. With children who have more skills or experience, we might say, "I notice that you can read all the words correctly" to highlight their accuracy, or "I notice you can read accurately and with expression" to praise their fluency. Then, in front of the child, we write what we have noted as their strength in our Pensieve, under the Strengths heading on the conferring sheet for that child. Just as the class will build the CAFE Menu board together, piece by piece, we will build our notes on individual children with them, so that over time they will assume responsibility for their goals and learning.

You may notice that when we talk to children in individual conferences, the language we use matches the phrasing that defines terms like *Accuracy* and *Fluency* on the CAFE Menu. Even in our first conference with a child, we are using the language on the menu, so that it becomes the common language our classroom community uses to talk about everyone's strengths and needs as readers.

Step 3: Set Goal and Identify Strategies with Student

Following the brief conversation regarding each child's strengths comes honest dialogue about goals: "One of the areas I am going to help you with to become a better reader this year is . . ." And then we fill in one of the four headings (Comprehension, Accuracy, Fluency, and Expand Vocabulary).

For example, if a child reads fluently but doesn't show much understanding of what he or she has read, we might say, "I noticed you read smoothly and with expression. One of the things that will help you become a better reader this year is to understand more of what you are reading. So your goal will be comprehension."

We then turn to that child's section in the Pensieve, which includes a copy of the CAFE Menu (Figure 3.3) and a goal sheet. We look together with the student at the list of strategies on the CAFE Menu under Comprehension and decide together on a next step.

We know that if students are struggling with comprehension, they may need *all* of the many strategies listed under that heading; however, when goal setting, we concentrate on only one or two strategies at a time in our conferences.

At this point, some of you are reading this and hoping we'll tell you *exactly* what strategy to pick for readers at that moment. As we confer

Figure 3.3 CAFE Menu

The Literacy CAFE Menu

Comprehension I understand what I read	**Accuracy** I can read the words	**Fluency** I can read accurately, with expression, and understand what I read	**Expand Vocabulary** I know, find, and use interesting words
Strategies Check for understanding Back up and reread Monitor and fix up Retell the story Use prior knowledge to connect with text Make a picture or mental image Ask questions throughout the reading process Predict what will happen; use text to confirm Infer and support with evidence Use text features (titles, headings, captions, graphic features) Summarize text; include sequence of main events Use main idea and supporting details to determine importance Determine and analyze author's purpose and support with text Recognize literacy elements (genre, plot, character, setting, problem/resolution, theme) Recognize and explain cause-and-effect relationships Compare and contrast within and between text	***Strategies*** Cross checking . . . Do the pictures and/or words look right? Do they sound right? Do they make sense? Use the pictures . . . Do the words and pictures match? Use beginning and ending sounds Blend sounds; stretch and reread Flip the sound Chunk letters and sounds together Skip the word, then come back Trade a word/guess a word that makes sense	***Strategies*** Voracious reading Read appropriate-level texts that are a good fit Reread text Practice common sight words and high-frequency words Adjust and apply different reading rates to match text Use punctuation to enhance phrasing and prosody (end marks, commas, etc.)	***Strategies*** Voracious reading Tune in to interesting words and use new vocabulary in speaking and writing Use pictures, illustrations, and diagrams Use word parts to determine the meaning of words (prefixes, suffixes, origins, abbreviations, etc.) Use prior knowledge and context to predict and confirm meaning Ask someone to define the word for you Use dictionaries, thesauruses, and glossaries as tools

Behaviors That Support Reading

Get started right away   Stay in one place   Work quietly   Read the whole time   Increase stamina   Select and read good-fit books

with students, how we wish for someone standing over our shoulder to do exactly that for us! The truth is there are many right strategies you can choose as you confer with children. If you've completed assessments, you will have some sense of what they are struggling with and what they might need.

The good news is that you don't have to make the perfect choice, or even the best choice, every time you confer. Why do we teachers put that much pressure on ourselves when teaching is such a complex art and science?

We choose a strategy for and with the children based on our best sense at the moment of what they need. Since we will check on their success with the strategy in our next conference, we can always adjust then, if necessary. If the strategy wasn't the right one for the student (perhaps it was too difficult, or it turned out to be one they already mastered), we figure that out together and pick a new strategy. Even if we were completely off-base, we and the student have learned something about his or her reading, and we can often learn from that error to improve our conferences with other students.

The point is to pick a strategy, give it a go, and then make sure we check back in to see if it is moving the child forward as a reader. For a look at some sample needs of our students and possible strategies, see From Assessment to Conferring: Sample Needs and Strategies in the appendix.

Here is another example of how it works. If we're working with a child who reads fluently but lacks some basic comprehension skills (a very common issue with our English language learner [ELL] classrooms), we might start with the Check for Understanding strategy. We introduce the strategy to the student by saying, "I think the strategy that might help you right now is Check for Understanding." Our language is explicit: "Your goal is going to be comprehension." Under the goal heading on the conferring sheet in the child's section of the Pensieve, we write "comprehension" in front of the child. We write the strategy Check for Understanding there as well.

Step 4: Student Declares Goal on Menu

The student takes a sticky note from the small basket we bring to conferences. (The notes are different colors and sizes, so that students can more easily pick out their writing on the CAFE Menu board.)

We have students write their names on sticky notes and place them under the goal heading Comprehension on the CAFE Menu board.

With older students, we also have them take out their reader's notebook or three-ring binder and have them mark their goal on their personal CAFE Menu with a highlighter and the date.

"Let's write your name on this sticky note."

Inna declares her goal by posting her name under the Comprehension heading on the CAFE Menu board.

Figure 3.4
Reading Conference form

Reading Conference

Strengths Accuracy and Fluency **Student** Inna

Goals and Strategies Comprehension Check for Understanding

Date / Touch Point	Observation and Instruction	Next Steps to Meet Goal
Date 1-8 **Touch Point**	Amber Brown Is Not a Crayon Sounds beautiful—No comprehension Teach—Model Check for Understanding	1. Think while reading 2. Stop at ends of paragraphs 3. Practice "I just read . . . Who, what Meet tomorrow
Date 1-9 **Touch Point**	Amber Brown · Stopped at end of paragraph Who Amber What . . . · Couldn't answer! · Went back to sentence level and reviewed who, what.	1. Stop and think while reading 2. Who . . . what . . . at end of each paragraph Meet tomorrow
Date 1-10 **Touch Point**	Amber Brown Difficult to remember Brought picture book The Incredible Adventures to help support meaning.	1. Read picture book 2. Read to Someone and practice ✓ for Understanding Tomorrow
Date 1-11 3 **Touch Point**	Reread Incredible Adventures . . . was able to ✓ for understanding at end of page Partner reading is helping Keep this up!	1. Read another picture book 2. Read to Someone. ✓ for Understanding Meet tomorrow
Date 1-12 3 **Touch Point**	Read Amber Brown 2nd day she is getting it even with chapter book Practice	1. Read Amber Brown 2. Read to Someone and ✓ for Understanding Meet every other day
Date 1-15 3 **Touch Point**	Amber Brown Able to ✓ for Under. by paragraph She said Read to Someone is helpful.	1. Amber Brown 2. Read to Someone 3. Sticky note 4. Begin writing in journal 2 examples of ✓ for Understanding Meet 2 day

Step 5: Teacher Fills Out Individual Reading Conference Form

While the child is placing his or her sticky note on the menu, we flip to the child's individual Reading Conference form (Figure 3.4). At the top of the form, we write the child's name, strengths, and goals. This form will help us keep track of our individual conferences and coaching sessions with each child.

Step 6: Teacher Fills Out Strategy Groups Form

After filling out the individual conferring sheet, we turn to the Strategy Groups section of our Pensieve. We ask ourselves, Is there anyone else we have assessed who needs this same goal and strategy? If there isn't, we write down "Goal: Comprehension" and

Strategy Groups and Instruction

Goal: Fluency	Strategy: Reread Text	Names	Touch Points
Date	**Lesson**		
1-17	Model—Shel Silverstein poem—Practice as a group	Katie	3
1-19	Review poem—Review strategy—practice		
1-23	Check group for good-fit books—students share reading their own stories.	Colin	4
1-25	Bring in poetry books, each choose and practice	Zach	3, 3
1-29	Partner Read and practice		
1-31	Most are getting this—make sure they have good-fit books	Josh	4, 4, 4
2-2	Students state their purpose for using this strategy		

Goal: Accuracy	Strategy: Use Beginning and Ending Sounds	Names	Touch Points
Date	**Lesson**		
1-15	Use Jack and Jill Nursery Rhyme—recite rhyme together—frame the word j-a-c-k. Look at beginning and ending sounds, do the same with Jill.	Nadjae	
		Haley	
1-16	Review beginning and ending sounds. Review Jack & Jill. Point and choose hill to frame and stretch each sound. Use leveled books with 1 sentence on each page—read and frame.	Colin	
1-17	Use Humpty Dumpty—recite poem—frame 2 words read together focusing on beginning and ending sounds. Review books from yesterday. Choral read. Choose 2 words to focus on beg. and end.	Donita	

Goal: Vocabulary	Strategy: Tune In to Interesting Words	Names	Touch Points
Date	**Lesson** 2/7 add—Use prior knowledge . . .		
1-10	Introduce word collectors—purpose—how to use. Add 2 words a day from their reading	Brandon	
1-17	Review word collectors—what do your words mean—how do you figure out the meaning	Ikman	
1-24	May need to add Use prior knowledge and context to predict and confirm meaning—review each word collector	Samuel	
2-7	Started layering on Use prior knowledge	Sandy	

Strategy Groups and Instruction

Goal: Comprehension	Strategy: Check for Understanding	Names	Touch Points
Date	**Lesson**		
1-10	Bring read-aloud to group—Model from today's readings, all practice	Sevilya	
1-11	Each practice in own book	Inna	3
1-12	I will call on each one during read-aloud to practice—How did it go?	Sandy	3, 4, 4
1-16	When do you use this strategy? Each share with group—give examples in own story	Juan	3
1-18	Partner group—practice with own stories with other person checking for understanding		

Goal: Accuracy	Strategy: Flip the Sounds	Names	Touch Points
Date	**Lesson**		
1-10	Whiteboard—Review long and short "a"—practice flipping	Jaeger	
1-11	Whiteboard—Review flipping sounds with "a"		
1-12	Whiteboard—Review long and short "i"—flip "i" and "a" words	Amanda	4, 4, 4
1-15	Whiteboard—Review "a" and "i" sounds find in own books		
1-16	Whiteboard—Review "o" sounds—flip each	Josh	
1-17	Whiteboard—Review a, i, o—flip and find in own books		
1-18	" —Review "e" sounds—flip each—practice	Haley	
1-19	" —Review a, e, i, o flip and find in books		
		Colin	3, 4

Goal: Comprehension	Strategy: Summarize Text; Include Sequence of Main Events	Names	Touch Points
Date	**Lesson**		
1-12	Define summary—model one verbally using the class read-aloud	Devon	
1-18	Sandy joined—review summarize, students share their own interpretation. I write in front of the group a summary from our read-aloud. Adding critical elements.	Brandon	
1-24	Partnered—each child tells the other a summary of their own book so far—in 4–5 sentences. Listen for main elements—Repeat back. Student writes summary from their own story—bring it back next time.	Simon	
		Sandy	

Figure 3.5 Sample Strategy Groups form

"Strategy: Check for Understanding" on the Strategy Groups form (see Figure 3.5) and start a list of students who would also benefit from this group. If this is not the first child with this goal and strategy, we merely add his or her name to the box labeled with this goal and strategy. This helps us keep track of our work with all our small groups.

Once children return from posting their names on the CAFE Menu bulletin board, we add the newly filled-out form to the Pensieve. We show students their section of the Pensieve and let them know we will be working together on their goals and strategies each time we meet with them and that this form will help us keep track of their learning. Before they leave us, we ask them to articulate their goals yet again. We are never surprised when students are unable to do this, even though they have just placed their names on the bulletin board. It may take a few times of working with and hearing their goals before they can internalize them.

Step 7: Instruction

This process is repeated with all students as we confer and set goals with them. Once we assess each child, we are ready to instruct, with the instruction truly being guided by each child's individual assessment. (For many examples of other goal-setting conferences and a more detailed explanation of the process, see Chapter 4, "Conferring with Children.")

Kids who have some background experience with the CAFE Menu may be able to articulate what they do well and sometimes what they need to work on in these first conferences. The tone and style of conferences with these more experienced CAFE-ers is a little different during the first week of school.

For example, Sebastian, who is eight years old and reads at about a fifth-grade reading level, said to Gail at his first conference of the year, "I'm really good at fluency." It was true, because he'd worked hard on fluency goals at the end of the previous school year.

Then he said, "But when I read, sometimes it doesn't make sense." Sebastian easily remembered the previous year's goals and successes, but it was hard for him to explain his needs as a reader beyond knowing he couldn't understand everything he was reading. Gail replied, "I noticed that same thing." We observed during the assessment that because he was so focused on fluency, he would read rapidly, dropping the final syllables of some words or making substitutions that made no sense just to keep up a rapid pace.

We explained that his goal would be accuracy, with Cross Checking as a strategy. What he was reading wasn't matching the words, and it wasn't making sense. Because Sebastian knew how the CAFE Menu worked, he independently wrote down his name on a sticky note and added it to the board under Accuracy.

Chapter 4

Conferring with Children: Principles and Examples

Just for fun when we're in a new classroom of young children together, we often introduce ourselves and begin by asking the class a question: "Who do you think is older?" Invariably, the children choose Gail. Why? Because she is a few inches taller than Joan.

For the record, Gail is a little older than Joan. (Joan is perpetually twenty-nine years old, and Gail is twenty-nine and a half.) The response always makes us smile and reminds us that assumptions made when we are young often prove to be wrong. As we grow, new experiences and learning have a profound effect on former assumptions.

As we've developed the CAFE Menu, we've had to change some of the assumptions we had about the best way to confer with students. Many of the assumptions we had when we were younger worked well, but it was a different environment for teaching, with different standards and accountability.

One of the biggest shifts when we began using the CAFE system in the beginning was getting up, moving about, and conferring with children one on one. We were accustomed to guided reading groups—staying in one area and having the children come to us for instruction. When we had time to confer individually, we'd call out for students to come to us or post a schedule of conferences on the board.

The concerns that we had, and that many teachers share, are about time and purposes. How long will each of these conferences take? How can we stay focused, given that there is so much we might tackle with each child? And what exactly is my role in the conference?

We've already written a bit about our conference procedures in the previous chapter on launching CAFE at the start of the school year. What we want to do now is give you a close-up view of the procedure we follow for all conferences, as well as examples of many different conferences with children of varying ability levels, so you can see how CAFE conferring works across grade levels.

Rethinking Conference Protocols

The reason we confer with students is to help them work toward individual goals. The goals come from the assessments at the start of the year or previous conferences, and they become the focus of each conference with the children.

While developing CAFE we resisted creating a preset conferring form. That's what we've become accustomed to as teachers—meeting with a child, and then filling in blanks on an assessment or conferring form as we listen to them read.

The conferring forms provided in many assessment systems or professional books often comprise a series of questions: What are you reading now? What are your strengths as a reader? Let's discuss vocabulary. What about fluency? Tell me why you chose this book. And on and on. Although these questions are valid, there are too many of them. By the time you've conferred with two or three children, the reading workshop for the day may be over.

Although keeping good records is an important component of CAFE, we've found that our time in the conference is best used observing and listening closely to the child, teaching and/or reinforcing the strategy he or she is working on, having the child practice the strategy, planning for the student's next step, and encouraging him or her to keep going. Our record-keeping forms are short, concise, and include only the information we need to refer to quickly to keep the child moving forward in reading. This way, instead of long conferences with detailed notes that may have little effect on the child's strategy work and immediate goal as a reader, we have continual brief, targeted contact and instruction with all of our students more frequently.

When we designed our initial conferring forms, they made complete sense to us. But we discovered that teachers across the country who were trying them varied greatly in their expertise and comfort level with conferring, and interpreted them in a variety of ways.

Gail's school had been studying how they could improve their work with at-risk students and increase their achievement. After much research, reflection, and working with their at-risk kids, along with hours of in-depth conversations, they decided that their schoolwide focus on improving work with their at-risk students would be individual conferring.

After this schoolwide decision, Gail was in a meeting with Janet, her assessment facilitator; Alene, her assistant principal; and Stan, her principal. In a candid conversation, Stan said, "If I was to confer with students, I would need a scaffold. We have been using the conferring forms and talking to teachers about how to assess and then meet with individuals, but that wouldn't be enough for me. I would need something more. What does the conference with a student look like? What would I need to pay attention to?"

His need was mirrored throughout the school. Teachers and instructional assistants were conferring with individual students and attempting to record their thinking. Yet when we met together to talk about their conferences, their work with children, and what they were writing, we noticed huge discrepancies in the recorded information. Their notebooks and recording of conferences were not similar in any way—sometimes nothing was written or a few words had been jotted down, whereas others had recorded a whole page.

What should a short, focused conference look like? What was most important to record when conferring with a child? Stan's candid questions made us sit up in our seats. Of course we knew what we were doing in the conferences and how to let our notes keep us focused for our valuable time with each student, but what about someone new to conferring? If teachers were expected to embrace conferences and to guide their students' progress, we needed to be more explicit about what the conferences looked like and how to let the Conferring Notebook support them.

The next twenty-four hours were a flurry of flying computer keys, scouring all our conference records from over the years, and poring over our current Conferring Notebooks. A clear pattern began to emerge as we studied our individual conferences.

Using our records as a model, combined with current research data, we added icons to our current form. The icons would serve as a scaffold or reminder of the structure we follow when conferring. This form is exactly the one we had originally designed and been using, but with a bit of visual support for teachers trying to master our techniques. The visually supported forms are designed to support teachers new to conferring without boxing others in, freeing them to get to the heart of the coaching and student learning.

Our conferences follow a similar structure each time (see Figure 4.1). The first icon is a pencil, which reminds us to jot down the title of the child's selection. The eye icon reminds us to observe what the student is doing related to the goal and to write that down. The brain icon is a reminder that it is time to think about what our focus for the conference will be. Do we teach what we previously planned or change the plan based on what we noticed in the student's reading today? This is also where we write down the focus of our conferring with the child.

The right side of the sheet refers to what our next steps will be with the student based on what we did today. The target icon reminds us to record the two things we want the student to work on until we meet with him or her again. The first always relates to comprehension, and the second is a strategy that relates to the student's specific, individualized reading goal. The "Next" arrow icon reminds us to talk to the student about when we will next meet to check on his or her progress and to schedule the appointment on the calendar in our Pensieve.

Figure 4.1 Gail's Reading Conference form with icons

Reading Conference with Icons

Strengths Listening Comprehension **Student** Jennie

Next Strategy?

Goals and Strategies Accuracy—Chunk Letters and Sounds Together

Date	Observation and Instruction	Next Steps to Meet Goal
Coaching Structure	Jot down the title of the selection. Observe . . . What do I notice related to the goal? Think :) . . . Do I teach or reinforce what we planned yesterday? Or change the plan based on what I see today?	Give child 2 "targets" each day 1. Comprehension—Think about your reading and what is happening in your selection. 2. Practice strategy. AND Next: Plan for tomorrow.
2/9 Sample	Jennie read <u>Super Fly Guy</u>. She came to 3 words she didn't know. She just guessed the words and went on. Teach her how to chunk sounds and letters together. Stop and check for understanding.	1. Think about what you are reading! 2. In your Reader's Notebook, log all the words you come across that you don't know and can use with this strategy. Next: Next, we will review the words in your notebook and watch you using this strategy in your reading. Let's set an appointment to meet back tomorrow. (Write on calendar.)
2/10 Sample	<u>Super Fly Guy</u> While reading came to 2 words, was able to chunk one word, could chunk the next word but couldn't "say it fast." Identified the word she read using the strategy. Restated how she used the strategy. Teach how to fix the last word by chunking sounds together.	1. Think about reading. 2. Continue to write words in notebook she is chunking. Next: Review notebook, see if she is transferring it to her reading.
2/11 Sample	<u>Space Race</u> Read fluently, came to the word "wrong" chunked and moved on. Seems like she has ahold of the strategy but not all words work with chunking. Watch for "flip the sound." She is not using the correct vowels. (<u>Shipes</u> for <u>Ships</u>) Modeled flip the sound with <u>ship</u>, so when chunking, she may need to flip until it makes sense.	1. Think about reading. Comprehend 2. Use a sticky note while reading to record the words she is using the strategy with. See if she can flip the sound if it doesn't make sense. Next: Check the notes and see if flipping the sound is helping with chunking.

These forms provide a bit more of the scaffolding and visual cues that Stan and teachers we've worked with have requested over the years.

This conference structure helps children look more closely at where they are now and where they might go tomorrow, or over the next week, as they work on skills and strategies to become better readers. Many of the conference protocols we've seen and used in the past look at what children are reading at the moment or ask them to talk about their whole life as readers, but that's not where the work and growth really occur. These forms and this conference structure enable us and our students to look beyond the moment to the concrete, practical steps that can be taken today, tomorrow, and this week to move students forward as readers. With CAFE, we are helping children become more independent in tracking their progress and taking responsibility for it.

One of the strengths of setting goals with children that they work on over a period of time is that it saves time in conferences. Instead of using a portion of each conference to determine a new goal or goals, the child begins with knowing he or she is working on developing fluency, or on expanding vocabulary. Starting with a focus, instead of always having to establish one at the beginning of the conference, saves an enormous amount of time. We can spend far more of the limited time we have with each child observing and listening to him or her read, and then providing focused, individualized instruction toward a predetermined goal.

A focus for our next conference is determined before we even meet with the child again. Once the structure is familiar, when children see us walking toward them for a conference, they mentally begin to sort through the progress they have made toward their goal and what topics they are prepared to discuss when we meet. We've also found that it's very hard for children to set meaningful reading goals without guidance or a concrete system. If you ask most children in the primary grades what their goal is as a reader, they are going to say, "I want to read chapter books." That goal isn't really going to move them forward in terms of understanding their strengths and needs as readers, and learning to monitor their reading growth independently.

Developing a shared language around reading development is a critical component of effective conferences. We can't use the core words *accuracy, fluency, comprehension*, and *expand vocabulary*, as well as the strategies within them, and expect students to use them as well, if they haven't become normal language in our learning community. We don't want our students to say, "I want to get farther along in the Accelerated Reader program." We don't actually use the Accelerated Reader program in our schools, but it's an example of how quickly students can come to equate a specific reading program with actual reading, which isn't necessarily the best thing for them to do. After all, how many of us as adults list "getting farther along in the Accelerated Reader program" as one of our literacy goals?

On the other hand, even as proficient readers we have a keen sense of struggling to comprehend certain technical texts (or poetry, for some of us). We can talk through different strategies we have for improving our reading of difficult texts, from Back Up and Reread to attending more to visual cues like graphs and headings.

In conferences, we're helping students become comfortable with words that describe their reading processes as they think about what it means to read and make progress as a reader, and those words aren't much different from the ones adults use. This becomes the language our classroom community shares as we talk about literacy.

Moving from Conferring to Coaching: A Shift in Thinking

When people started asking us to share what our conferences with children looked and sounded like, we had to step back and become more conscious of what we did automatically when conferring with students. So we began to take notes—recording exactly what we did and said—and emailed them back and forth to each other. As we pored over these notes, a common thread became apparent: we weren't focusing as much on what books students were reading, or when they thought they would finish them. These are the areas we focused on in informal conferences during reading workshops in years

Joan holds a one-on-one coaching conference with Treven.

Figure 4.2
Coaching Toward a Target

Coaching Toward a Target

Productive, Effective, Focused Teaching and Learning

1. Check calendar for appointments.
2. Prepare (30 seconds)
   Review your conferring notes for the student's strengths and strategy focus.
3. Observe (1 minute) *"[Student], please read so I can listen in; then tell me about yourself as a reader."*
   Observe the student. Is he or she applying the skill/strategy taught or reinforced last time you met?
   What is the student doing well with his or her strategy/skill application?
   Record this on the conferring sheet.
4. Reinforce and Teach (1 minute)
   "I noticed _______; what did you notice? Today we are going to _______."
   Verbally share with student your observations of what he or she was doing well.
   Teach or reinforce the skill or strategy you feel is just right for the student now by
   - explicit explanation,
   - modeling,
   - thinking aloud,
   - offering advice.
5. Practice (1 minute) *"Now it is your turn. You try . . . "*
   Ask the student to practice the skill/strategy while you listen in.
6. Plan (30 seconds) *"This is what I am hearing, and because of that, this may be our next step."*
   Based on today's teaching and learning, decide and agree together what the next step will be. It isn't uncommon for students to need continued practice with the previous strategy.
   Write this plan on the coaching sheet.
7. Encourage (15 seconds)
   Just before you leave the student, encourage him or her to continue to practice the skill taught or reinforced today.
   Student should articulate the goal.

- The times above serve as guidelines, and though it isn't necessary to strictly adhere to them, they will give you a general idea so you can keep your conferences focused and brief.
- Each step above may be shorter or longer, depending on what the child is doing that day, and where you are in the gradual release of teaching the skills or strategies to the student.
- Remember that brief, focused conferences that occur frequently are considerably more beneficial than sporadic, lengthy ones.

past. We realize we've shifted, so that our conferences are now more like coaching sessions, based on the child's individual goal and strategy.

This reflection and new awareness led to a newly defined purpose and title for our conferring session, "Coaching Toward a Target—Productive, Effective, Focused Teaching and Learning," and a remodeled set of conferring guidelines (Figure 4.2).

The focused, purposeful, assessment-driven conferences were leading to exciting growth in our students' lives, and colleagues who were trying out the new conferring form appreciated the new focus. The first guide sheet had no expectations written on it for time spent on each step, and colleagues were finding that they didn't have time for more than a conference or two during a workshop. We realized they must be spending more time than we were on the steps, so we established a rough estimate of how much time each step should take and added it to the form.

The time frame on the form Coaching Toward a Target is a guide for those who are trying to streamline their conferences, but it isn't meant to be adhered to religiously. We are aware that your times will vary a bit, depending on the child you are conferring with and what you are working on, just as they do in our rooms.

The Seven Elements of Successful Conferences

Like most of the materials in this book, the guidelines for conferring are simply that—guidelines—and we've found it helpful to refer to them when we have a conference that meanders far away from the original goal or leaves a student with a vague sense that things didn't go as well as they should have. At that point, we look back at the conferring guidelines and often realize we made a big mistake, rushing through or skipping an element or going off track in some other way. We have found that adhering to the guidelines keeps our conferences intentional, focused, and successful. Following is the format we strive to use.

Figure 4.3 Joan's calendar

January

Sunday	Monday	Tuesday	Wednesday	Thursday	Friday	Saturday
	1	2 Amanda	3 Juan Katie Mahesh	4 Ikman Haley	5 Juan Katie Mahesh	6
7	8 Serilya Inna	9 Serilya Inna Haley	10 Serilya Inna	11 Serilya Inna	12 Inna Jaeger	13
14	15 Inna Jaeger	16 Colin Carlos	17 Inna Josh	18 Julia Devon	19 Mahesh Nadjae	20
21	22 Colin Josh Devon Nadjae	23 Sandy Simon	24 Serilya Devon Zach	25 Sandy Samuel Brandon	26 Serilya Simon Brandon	27
28	29 Colin Devon	30 Donita Zach	31 Donita			

Step 1: Check the Calendar for Appointments

We use the calendar (Figure 4.3) in the Pensieve to make appointments with children that we're keeping an eye on, so the first thing we do when we're ready to start conferring for the day is open the notebook

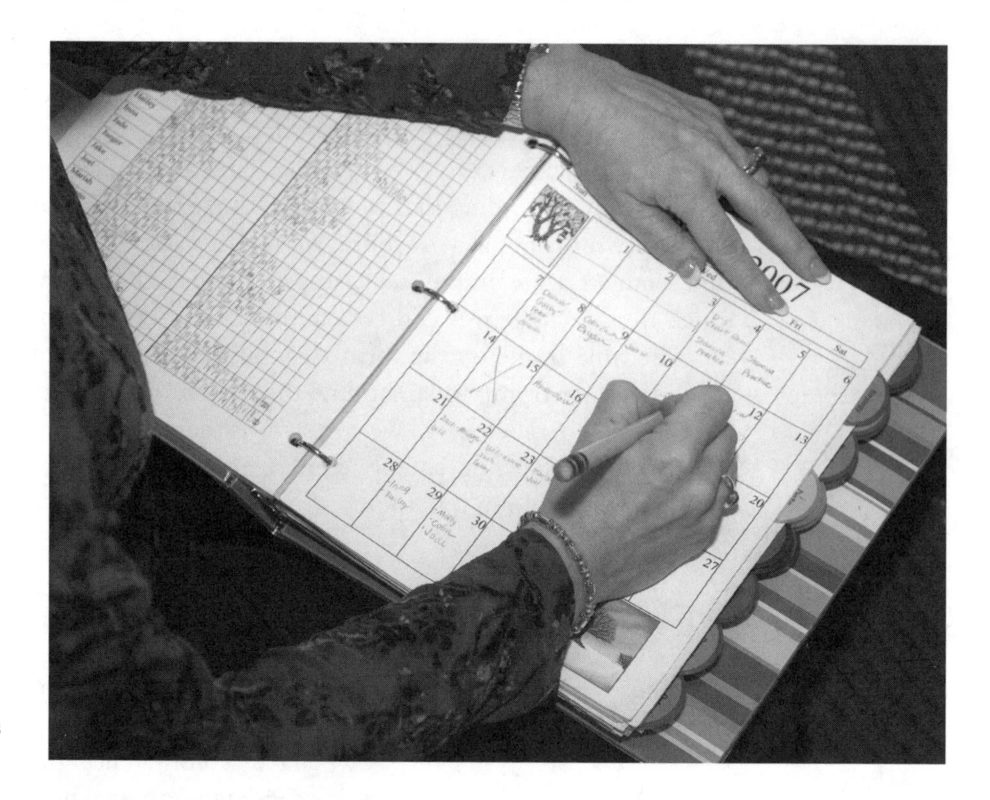

Joan checks the calendar for appointments.

Figure 4.4 Gail's Keeping Track form

Keeping Track: Reading Writing

	Reading												Writing											
Amanda	11/2	11/5	11/10	11/15	11/16	11/19	11/24	11/26	11/31															
Brandon	11/2	11/4	11/8	11/9	11/16	11/19	11/24	11/29	11/31															
Carlos	11/2	11/4	11/9	11/10	11/16	11/19	11/25	11/29	11/31															
Colin	11/2	11/4	11/8	11/10	11/16	11/22	11/25	11/29	11/31															
Devon	11/2	11/8	11/12	11/18	11/22	11/27	11/3																	
Donita	11/12	11/18	11/25																					
Haley	11/2	11/9	11/10	11/16	11/19	11/25	11/30																	
Ikman	11/4	11/11	11/18	11/25																				
Inna	11/8	11/9	11/10	11/11	11/15	11/17	11/19	11/26	11/31															
Jaeger	11/12	11/15	11/22	11/29																				
Josh	11/9	11/16	11/23	11/30																				
Juan	11/3	11/10	11/17	11/24	11/31																			
Julia	11/4	11/12	11/18	11/26																				
Katie	11/3	11/5	11/8	11/12	11/17	11/23	11/24	11/30	11/31															
Mahesh	11/3	11/5	11/8	11/12	11/18	11/23	11/24	11/30																
Nadjae	11/5	11/8	11/11	11/12	11/15	11/17	11/19	11/22	11/24	11/26	11/30													
Samuel	11/3	11/5	11/9	11/15	11/18	11/23	11/25	11/30																
Sandy	11/3	11/8	11/9	11/15	11/17	11/23	11/25	11/30																
Sevilya	11/8	11/9	11/10	11/11	11/18	11/24	11/26	11/30																
Simon	11/3	11/8	11/9	11/15	11/17	11/24	11/26	11/30																
Zach	11/3	11/8	11/9	11/15	11/17	11/23	11/25	11/29	11/30	11/31														

and check it for scheduled appointments. Not every child is going to have an appointment listed every day, or even every other day; on any given day, there are usually only two or three children we must confer with. If we do have an appointment listed, we're going to start with one of those children.

If we don't have any appointments or have already met with the children listed, we can look at our Keeping Track form (Figure 4.4) to scan for children we haven't met with for a while. We strongly believe that fair isn't always equal with children—some children need more conferring than others, especially at certain crucial points in their development as readers. Our more at-risk students will have more boxes filled on the keeping-track form than our higher-functioning students, because they need

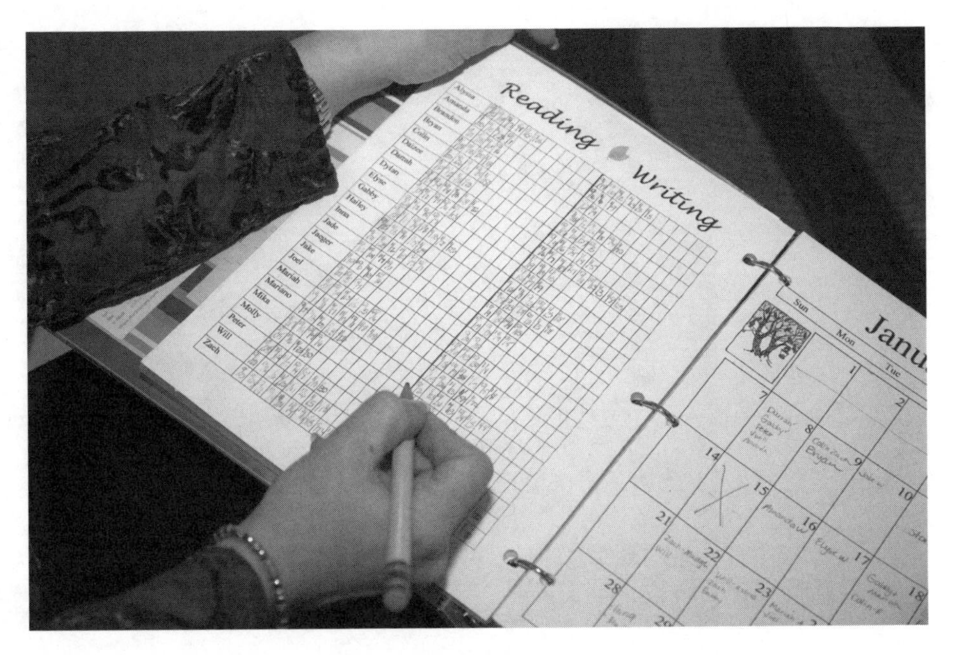

Joan keeps track of conferences on the Keeping Track form.

more one-on-one time with us. The Keeping Track form works in concert with the calendar as we organize our time and make choices about who needs time with us on any given day.

At the same time, we also realized when we developed and started using these forms that we were neglecting some of our highest-functioning students because we were conferring so often with our most needy learners. It's easy if we aren't keeping track to go two or three weeks without meeting with those quiet and capable students who will never ask for your attention—and that isn't fair to them. Even Tiger Woods needs a coach, and all students benefit from the focused one-on-one attention and goal setting that come from conferring. As we scan the Keeping Track form, we are keeping an eye out for these students who are easy to overlook because they read and write so well.

Step 2: Prepare for the Conference

After we've decided who we're going to meet with, we open our Pensieve to that child's section of the notebook to see what we did with them the last time we met.

During this quick scan of our notes, we look for the following information from the last conference: What was our teaching point? What was the takeaway (or follow-up) the child should be working on between conferences?

"Let's see what we worked on with you last time."

This information is foremost in our minds as we join the child. We're focused strictly on what happened in the last conference, because we're realistic. We want to spend the bulk of our time conferring, not poring over notes from previous conferences. This quick preparation gives the conference a clear sense of direction from the beginning.

As you prepare to confer with a child, always keep in mind that the times on the guide sheet for each element are just general suggestions—we don't really use a stopwatch. We want to take Debbie Miller's advice to heart:

> *It's true that teachers have never been under more pressure. We're bombarded by demands and directives deemed by others as necessary and non-negotiable. As a result, teachers everywhere are making Herculean efforts to fit everything in. It's no wonder there's talk by some of hurry-up-and-get-it-done.*
>
> *But when getting done takes precedence over the doing, when finishing becomes more important than the figuring out, we've lost sight of why we became teachers in the first place.* (2008, 106)

We want students to have the sense that we are completely present with them, truly focused on their reading and their needs, and that we have all the time in the world to figure it out together. Taking just a few moments before we meet with a student to scan our notes from the previous conference enables us to start calmly and purposefully, instead of frantically shuffling through papers and trying to remember where we are. Because the plan was made the last time we were together, we just have to refresh our memories by glancing at the form.

Step 3: Observe Child and Listen to Reading

After reviewing our notes, we hunker down wherever the student is working to confer. This may be on the rug in the meeting area, on a couch in the class library, or at work tables near the sink.

We used to call students to come to us for a conference, but calling out to a child disrupted the productive atmosphere we were trying to foster for independent work. "Susan, come here. Suuuuusan, over here for your conference. Yoo-hoo! Has anyone seen Susan?" Words like these disrupt not only Susan, but everyone else in the room.

Walking to the child provides us with enough time to review our notes from the last conference and an opportunity to watch, giving us a snapshot of that child during literacy workshop. Is Susan reading or writing? Where does she choose to sit? Who is she sitting by? This lightning-quick observation gives us more useful information about who each child is not just as a reader, but as a member of our classroom community. En route, we also can use this time to tap a distracted child on the shoulder or to nod enthusiastically at a child who is excited about his or her new book, without even breaking stride.

Joan joins Peter, who is doing Read to Self, at a table for a conference.

Sometimes the floor is the most convenient place for a conference.

Once we reach the child, the first thing we usually say to him or her is "I see that you're reading. Would you read so I can listen in?" As we noted in Chapter 2 on launching the school year with CAFE, our very first conferences of the year with each child include a battery of required school and district assessments. That's just the reality of school life early in the year. Once we are past those first required assessments, we want to get into the routine of students expecting that in every conference they will read a bit to us, talk about their reading, and assess their progress toward their goal.

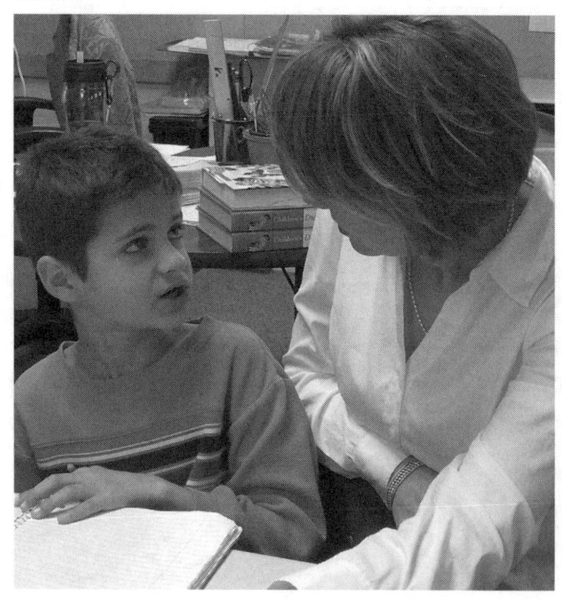
Sitting at a student's desk is another place to confer.

While we're listening to the children read, we're seeing whether they are applying the strategies toward a goal we worked on in the previous conference. We can't throw too many teaching points at them at once, so we're very focused on those one or two strategies they have declared as being of value in helping them reach their goal or goals. After observing, we write down on our form what text they were reading and add some notes related to their goal. For example, were they able to check for understanding? Did they choose to back up and reread?

Step 4: Reinforce and Teach

Once we've noticed whether the student is able to apply the skill or strategy, we have a decision to make. What is the one thing we should teach this child today? We have lots of choices. We might continue with the same goal and strategy, or we might adjust it based on what we've observed thus far.

We always begin by telling children what we've noticed about them as readers. Then we teach by giving an explicit explanation of a strategy and modeling it for them, or we can talk about the strategies in specific ways, in relation to the texts they are reading.

This conference moment, when we are trying to move a child forward just a little bit as a reader every time we meet, is where true coaching and teaching comes in. It's not assessment—that takes place daily as we quietly observe the student reading and working without us. It's not a broad interview about their interests as readers. It's the brief time we need to figure out exactly where the child is in terms of mastering a strategy, and what scaffold that child needs to keep growing. In Coaching Toward a Target, we list this time as roughly one minute, because it is short. We keep the general guideline of one minute in our heads mostly because we don't want to overwhelm the child. When our conferences fail, it's often because we've tried to teach the child too many skills or strategies and have succeeded only in confusing him or her. There are many examples of specific instruction in conferences later in this chapter.

Step 5: Practice the Strategy

After we've met with a child and reinforced the goal and strategy, or taught a new one, we observe him or her practice. This gives us a chance to see whether the child really understood what we've taught and whether he or she needs more coaching or support. If you've ever watched a coach in a practice session, you've seen how most sessions are a mix of demonstrating a new skill, watching team members practice, and then fine-tuning the skill with further instruction in the midst of practice. Musicians go through a similar process as their instructor works with them.

Once we listen to the child practice, we can modify our instruction to improve understanding of the skill. Sometimes we discover that there are very basic misunderstandings between what we asked for (or expected) and what the child perceived as the task or activity. This is the beauty of one-on-one conferring. If we're doing just whole-group instruction or just working with small groups, we are less likely to see with clarity what individual children understand and can apply from our lessons. We often take our learning from this part of the conference to determine what lessons we might want to teach to the whole class or in small groups, if the same issues are emerging with multiple students.

Step 6: Plan

Once the child has read to us and practiced the strategy, and we're confident he or she is ready for independent work, we usually say, "This is what I'm hearing" or "This is what I'm seeing you do. This is what I think our next step should be." If the child has really mastered the skill he or she has been working on, we're ready to move on to a new strategy.

How do we determine whether we're ready to move on? We look for four or five touch points of demonstrating the strategy successfully. Touch points are when we see students exhibiting the behaviors of the strategy they have been practicing, using their own books. Typically we either make note of the date the child successfully used the strategy or put a check mark in the touch point column of the conferring sheet. Once the child has four or five touch points demonstrating his or her use of the strategy, we highlight and date this strategy on the student's CAFE Menu, located in his or her section of the Pensieve. We also place a check mark and date in the date or data point box located on the conferring form or the strategy-group page denoting the end to the teaching and coaching support for this particular strategy. With the child and the CAFE Menu in front of us, we decide on the next area to highlight and practice.

For grading purposes (if we had to assign a grade), we would use either the alphabetical system or a standards-based system to put the student's grade on the conferring form instead of a check mark.

Often in conferences, children demonstrate that they are approaching competence but still need more practice. Continued practice can take many forms. Depending on the strategy, we may ask them to use sticky notes to mark their thinking so we can see what's going on in their heads, or we might ask them to use their reader's notebook to get their thinking process down in a narrative form.

Even though the practice looks different for different children, all children are expected to work independently between conferences on a particular skill or strategy. After deciding on a plan of action, we talk about when we will meet with them next. If they need considerable support, we often plan to meet with them again the next day or even later the same day during the workshop. If we're meeting with them the next day, we mark the appointment on our calendar. If they are starting to demonstrate the skill or strategy with some proficiency, then we might schedule an appointment for two or three days later.

We may not need to write down an appointment at all if we've decided we'll meet in a week or so (this is often the case with more proficient readers working on a more sophisticated strategy over time). We don't need to write a specific time down for a conference the following week, because our Keeping Track form ensures we never go longer than that before meeting with any student.

The time spent deciding when the next conference will take place is as much for us as it is for the students. We used to promise often to meet with a child the next day, and we'd forget. We don't even want to think about what that did to the development of so many of the young readers in our care over the years! The calendar holds us accountable as well as the students, and we both share the responsibility of being ready for our next conference, whenever we've agreed that will take place.

Our sense of what it means for students to be accountable for their learning is probably the biggest shift in our thinking as a result of CAFE. Years ago, we had written assignments, and that's how children were held accountable—they completed the worksheets or forms, or we checked off that they'd completed the required number of pages in their reading logs. We now believe ultimate accountability comes while meeting one on one with students, and seeing in that moment whether children can apply to a self-selected text what has been taught. When we agree to a day and time for the next meeting, it's a concrete reminder that they are accountable for completing the practice we've agreed on until the next conference.

Step 7: Encourage

This last step is easy to forget in the rush of trying to get everything done, but it is crucial to the conference. We always take a moment to pause with students and savor their growth. It's an "Attaboy" or "Attagirl" moment: "You're doing so well—look at the progress you've made! Now get back in there and learn some more."

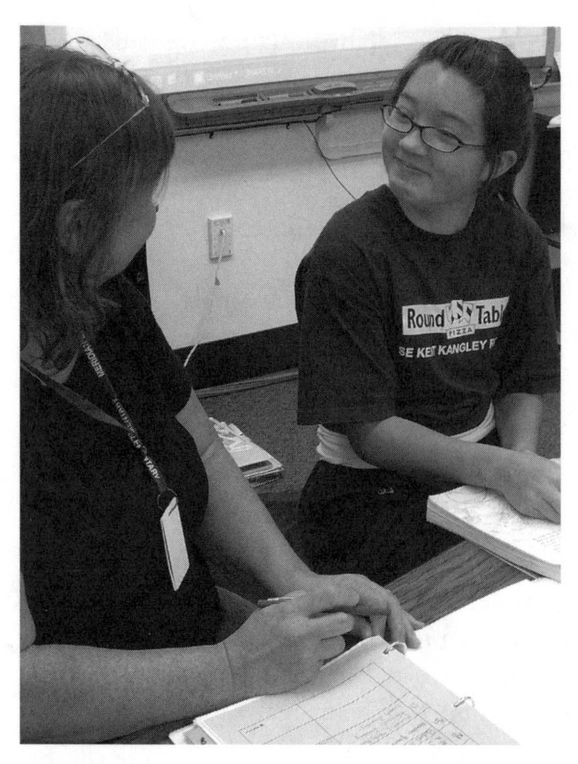

Encourage: "Look how well you are doing. Keep going!"

These final words, which are specific to the text and strategy the child has been working on, are the imprint we leave with that child of how we see him or her as a learner.

The last moments of the conference are given over to the children articulating the goals or strategies they are working on. It can't be a secret from them—they need to gain the sense of power, responsibility, and growth that comes from taking charge of their learning.

Okay, we know we have mentioned the importance of being flexible many times already, but we want to reiterate that a one-minute teaching point may last three minutes with us—or fifteen seconds. The last thing we want is for you to get knotted up in watching the clock (or even worse, carrying a stopwatch with you), worrying about how much time you are spending conferring rather than being completely present and attending to the student you are with. Allow the conference form to help you keep the conference focused and brief.

We observe and listen closely during conferences.

Reinforcing and teaching are the fourth step of the process.

Planning for the next step saves time at the next conference.

We used to have lengthy conferences with just a small number of students each week, so we rarely got to all children in just a few days as we do now. You will see as you move to short, focused conferences that it actually feels like less of a time crunch. We know we will have the time to get to all children routinely now, at least every two to three days, and even more important, we will get to the children each day who need our attention most by making and keeping appointments with them using the calendar.

Setting a new goal comes at the end of the one-on-one session.

The next chapter presents a series of snapshots of different conferences with children across the elementary grades who are all working on a range of strategies. You'll quickly see that there is no one right way to present any of the CAFE strategies, and how flexible the seven-step process is in any conferring situation.

Eavesdropping on Some Conferences

Goal: Comprehension

Strategy: Check for Understanding (Beginning Reader)

We had a reading appointment for Sevilya on our calendar one day. She was a beginning English language learner who learned her letters and sounds rapidly and could decode easily. We had just finished her assessment and noted in our Pensieve that she didn't stop to check for understanding. Comprehension became her goal, and Check for Understanding would be the strategy of focus (see Figure 5.1).

"Hi, Sevilya. Yesterday we read together to find out about you as a reader and to set your reading goal. Do you remember what you are really good at?" Like many of our younger students, Sevilya didn't remember her strengths and goals after hearing them once. We understand and accept that we'll have to remind some students several times what their goals and strengths are.

"Sevilya, you are great at accuracy—that means you can read the words correctly! Right now your main goal is comprehension. I am going to help you learn to monitor your meaning and check for under-

Gail confers with Sevilya about using the strategy Check for Understanding.

Figure 5.1 Gail's Reading Conference form for Sevilya

Reading Conference

Strengths Accuracy **Student** Sevilya

Goals and Strategies Comprehension—Check for Understanding

Date / Touch Point	Observation and Instruction	Next Steps to Meet Goal
Date 1-9 **Touch Point**	Danny's Timeline Read all words accurately Modeled Check for Understanding She practiced	1. Think while reading 2. Use sticky note to mark where she Checks for Understanding Meet tomorrow
Date 1-10 **Touch Point**	What Do You Do with a Tail Like This? Reading accurately, not stopping to Check for Understanding. Went through sticky notes from yesterday. Able to Check for Understanding.	1. Stop at end of each page to Check for Understanding. 2. Mark with sticky Meet tomorrow
Date 1-11 3 **Touch Point**	Quill Stopped 2 times to think and tell about story. Looked at sticky notes. She explained each.	1. Comp—Continue sticky notes to mark times she Checks for Understanding 2. Comp—think Next: Try reading a passage to her
Date 1-15 3 **Touch Point**	Quill Is Busy. Stopped and discussed story. Starting to practice with purpose. I read would you could you, stopped and modeled Check for Understanding, then she did.	1. Comp—continue sticky notes 2. Call on her during read aloud to ✓ for Understanding Continue to gradually release. Meet in 2 days.
Date **Touch Point**		
Date **Touch Point**		

standing. I have been talking about this when I read stories to the class—have you noticed? Let me show you what it looks like and sounds like."

We then picked up a short book from Sevilya's book box. It had one line per page and an illustration that supported the text. Because this book was so short, we read five pages (until we were about halfway through the book) before stopping. Then, turning to Sevilya, we said, "Now I'm going to check for understanding before I continue to read." Because the book was very simple, we did a quick retelling of the story and then said, "See how I remember what I just read, so that now I can move on to the rest of the story?"

We finished the rest of the story, and then stopped again and checked for understanding. This time we modeled not being able to remember the story correctly. "Sevilya, if I don't remember the story correctly, I'm not finished reading. I need to back up and reread that part. Remember that the secret to monitoring for meaning is to think about the story while we read? We can't just say the words! Now let's have you try."

Sevilya took another book from her book box, opened it, and began to read, stopping to check for understanding. She turned to us and said, "How come no one ever told me I was supposed to think about the words I read?"

"It sure does help make reading fun when we understand what we read, doesn't it? Great work on this strategy, Sevilya. I'm going to make an appointment with you in my calendar for tomorrow so we can meet and continue working on Check for Understanding. For the rest of Daily Five today and tomorrow, I want you to keep reading and stopping to check for understanding. Here's a stack of stickies. Each time you stop to check for understanding, put one on the edge of the book and we'll look at sticky notes together tomorrow. Can you tell me again what your goal and strategy are?"

Sevilya was a new reader and brand new to goal setting and strategy work. She was unable to tell us what her goal was, but did know that she was going to stop to check for understanding so that what she read made sense. We end every conference with asking kids to tell us again what their goal and strategy are. After all, it is their reading, their goal, and their strategy, not ours. They need to internalize them, and the best way to accomplish that is through constant reminders and articulation.

"I can't wait to meet with you tomorrow, Sevilya. Great job with Check for Understanding today. Keep going!"

Goal: Comprehension

Strategy: Check for Understanding (Advanced Reader)

Inna, an English language learner in our third-grade class, could read anything you put in front of her. She could decode beautifully and had an uncanny ability to read fluently and with expression even though she didn't understand the majority of what she was reading. Inna's biggest challenge was that she had no idea that her meaning was breaking down. Because of this, she was considered a struggling reader and one we would be meeting with daily to coach in this area.

We sat down beside her and listened to her read a bit. Then we began. "Inna, do you remember what you are really good at as a reader?"

She smiled proudly and even stuck her chest out a bit as she responded, "I can read all the words right. I am a great reader!"

"You are absolutely correct—you can read the words right. Do you remember what your goal is?"

Inna could not remember what her goal was.

"Your goal is comprehension, which means that you need to understand what you read. The strategy I will be teaching you first is called Check for Understanding. I have been talking about this in class each day when I read to you. I am so excited for you to learn how to use this strategy so you can know what the author is telling you in the stories you read. Let me show you how to do this strategy using this picture book."

Because Inna could decode anything, her heart's desire (like most eight-year-olds) was to read a chapter book. However, we moved her out of chapter books and into picture books with rich illustrations that would support the vocabulary and story line. These were the kinds of texts she needed, with more supports for understanding the text and vocabulary in it.

We presented her with a large pile of enticing picture books, each with two to five sentences of text per page and beautiful illustrations that we were sure would capture her interest.

"Inna, which one of these books would you like to read right now?" Inna chose a particularly lovely book with detailed illustrations for the conference.

"Inna, I'm going to model for you the strategy Check for Understanding." Because English is her second language, we read just one page with three sentences on it. Then we stopped and did a short retelling, saying, "I just read. . . ."

"Inna, let's have you try the next page." She read the page beautifully, but when we asked, "Can you check for understanding?" she looked at us with a blank stare. We prompted her with "What you say is 'I just read. . . .'" Again, a blank stare.

We read the page to her and said, "Let's have you try this. When you come to the end of one page, say to yourself, 'Who and what? Who did I just read about? And what just happened?'" We modeled this "who and what" technique for her after reading the next page. There was a glimmer in her eye as she said, "I can do that!"

She read the next page, and as she came to the end of it, she said to herself, "Who and what." She was able to tell us the "who" on the page and then what the character was doing. We turned to the next page. We read it aloud, then stopped and checked for understanding by saying "who and what."

Inna read the next page, which was longer. When she got to the end, she couldn't remember the "who and what" from the story.

"Inna, this time you couldn't remember the 'who and what' after reading the whole page. Try reading just part of the page, stop to check for understanding, read the rest of the page, and then stop again to check the 'who and what.' Let me show you what that looks like."

We modeled reading the longer page, stopping partway through, checking for understanding with the "who and what" technique, then reading the rest of the page and checking for understanding again.

"Inna, tell me again what your goal is." This time she could articulate her goal and even what it meant!

"Inna, I want you to practice this strategy of Check for Understanding, answering 'who and what,' during Read to Self or Read to Someone workshop times. I'm going to make an appointment with you for tomorrow on the calendar. At that time, you'll show me the pages you read, and share how the strategy of Check for Understanding answering the 'who and what' questions worked."

We wrote her name on the calendar page in our Pensieve and sent her off to practice, knowing that we had made a small step in the right direction. Daily work with Inna would be required to move her from the rudimentary level of Check for Understanding answering "who and what" and into more sophisticated strategies of monitoring her meaning.

Goal: Accuracy

Strategy: Flip the Sound (Beginning Reader)

Jaeger was a seven-year-old who was beginning to crack the reading code. He had excellent listening comprehension skills and a wonderful vocabulary. Jaeger knew all the letter sounds in isolation. When he came to a word he didn't know, he would attempt to read it accurately. If he read the word wrong and it didn't make sense, he would try again, making the same error over and over.

For example, Jaeger was reading a book and came to the word *stop*. He pronounced it *stope*. It is common for beginning readers to try the long-vowel sound first. Jaeger knew the word *stope* didn't make sense in the sentence "The boy tried to stope the ball." So he smartly used the strategy of Back Up and Reread. Again, he read the word *stop* as *stope*. He knew it didn't make sense, so he backed up and reread again. This continued until he finally accepted that he couldn't figure out the word, so he just skipped it and read on.

When Jaeger came to the end of the page, we asked him to go back and read the sentence again. He said, "That didn't make sense." He even knew which word didn't make sense. We then placed our palm down on the table beside him and, using this as the visual cue, began to teach him the strategy of Flip the Sound (see Figure 5.2).

"Jaeger, you have such wonderful comprehension that when you read that sentence, you knew this word [pointing to *stop*] didn't make sense. You did just the right thing; you backed up and reread it. However, you read the word the exact same way, and it still didn't make sense. I'm going to show you a new Accuracy strategy that might be a good one for you to try when you come to a word you don't know. It's called Flip the Sound." As soon as we labeled the strategy, we turned our hand over so the palm was up, in a flipping motion.

"Let me show you how it works. If I was reading this sentence like you did and realized that the word *stope* didn't make sense, yet it looked right because I cross-checked it, I would want to try going back and asking myself what other sounds the letters could make. I'll take the other sounds and flip them [making hand motion], listening to see if they make a new word that makes sense. Let's see, *stope*. I know *s* and *t* say /st/, and I know that *o* is a vowel and vowels usually make more than one sound. I'm going to try reading the word again and flipping the vowel sound." We reread it, and when we came to the word *stop*, we flipped our hand over as we flipped the *o* from the long-vowel to the short-vowel sound. "I recognize the word *stop* and it makes sense in the sentence! I flipped the /o/ sound so the word went from *stope* to *stop*. Let's read some more of this book and I'll model Flip the Sound again for you."

After modeling with Jaeger's book, we took out a small whiteboard and wrote some words on it, such as *bat, it, run*, and *go*. He could easily read each word, but we asked him to flip the vowel sound anyway, to begin training his ear to listen for when the word he reads makes sense.

"Jaeger, here are a couple of sticky notes. When you are reading today, I want you to give this strategy a try and mark those words with a sticky

Figure 5.2 Joan's Reading Conference form for Jaeger

Reading Conference

Strengths Listening Comprehension **Student** Jaeger

Goals and Strategies Accuracy—Flip the Sound

Date Touch Point	Observation and Instruction	Next Steps to Meet Goal
Date 1-12 **Touch Point**	Read In My House Read only short vowels Teach long vowels for "a." Use white-board. Review long and short "a"—then flip the sounds.	1. Think while reading 2. Sticky note words that have a short "a" sound. Read to me tomorrow Meet tomorrow
Date 1-13 **Touch Point**	Read The Bat Brought 2 sticky notes—read short "a" words then practiced flipping the sound and asking—Does that word make sense in the story?	1. Think while reading 2. Sticky note "a" words Meet with group tomorrow
Date 1-17 **Touch Point**	Read Danny's Party Showed words that had an "a"—we flipped sounds together. Does it makes sense? Used whiteboard to practice flipping sounds.	1. Think 2. Sticky words you can flip. Introduce "i" sounds and flip—Tomorrow!
Date **Touch Point**		
Date **Touch Point**		
Date **Touch Point**		

note. Let's set an appointment with you for tomorrow and work some more on Flip the Sound." We wrote his name on the appointment calendar in our Pensieve.

Goal: Accuracy

Strategy: Flip the Sound (Advanced Reader)

When we met with Amanda, an advanced reader in the same class, she was experiencing similar difficulties with reading words accurately. The difference was that Amanda was reading words that were longer and

Figure 5.3 Reading Conference form with icons for Amanda

Reading Conference with Icons

Strengths Fluency **Student** Amanda

Goals and Strategies Accuracy Flip the Sound; Comprehension—Monitor and Fix Up

Date / Touch Point	Observation and Instruction	Next Steps to Meet Goal
1-10 Touch Point	Gollywhopper Games Reads words incorrectly—Keeps reading Stop—Does that makes sense? Flip the Sound until it does	1. Tune in to the word that doesn't make sense 2. Jot word in notebook Next: Meet 3 days
1-15 1 Touch Point	Gollywhopper Games No words written in notebook She read aloud a paragraph. We practiced together—wrote word.	1. Tune in to words when it doesn't make sense. 2. Write in notebook! Next: Meet tomorrow
1-16 2 Touch Point	Gollywhopper Games One word in notebook—muttered—reread paragraph Could flip sound and it made sense.	1. Tune in to words 2. Keep words in notebook. Next: 3 days
Touch Point		Next
Touch Point		Next
Touch Point		Next

more complex. When she read this sentence from *The Gollywhopper Games* by Jody Feldman, "On a shining wooden floor stood a massive wooden table surrounded by sixteen burgundy leather chairs," she read the word *massive* as *mase-ive*. She's an advanced reader, so she knew to stop, back up, and try again. This time when she reached the word *massive*, she tried to break the word into smaller chunks, a great strategy, but she neglected to flip the vowel sound from the long /a/ to short /a/. This was a perfect opportunity to stop Amanda and teach her the strategy of Flip the Sound (see Figure 5.3).

Whether the child is a beginning reader like Jaeger or an advanced reader like Amanda, we follow the same sequence to teach this strategy:

- Model using a word the child has read within his or her text.
- Continue modeling a few times from the child's text.
- Using a whiteboard or words in the text, have the child practice Flip the Sound a few times.
- Assign the child the task of practicing the strategy during Read to Self, recording the words practiced on either a sticky note or in their reader's notebook.
- Set an appointment to review their use of the strategy and reinforce the lesson.

Goal: Comprehension

Strategy: Summarize Text (Advanced Reader)

When conferring with an advanced reader, we don't assign the strategy of summarizing text until the child has command over Retell the Story and Check for Understanding. Once these are in place, advanced readers may have the goal of comprehension with the strategy of summarizing for a long time.

Devon was one of those students. A sixth-grade advanced reader, Devon could decode and read fluently with ease. He had a strong vocabulary both in his native language and in English. He was in a place as a reader where the goals of continuing to build vocabulary and fine-tune his comprehension would be ones he stuck with for an extended period of time. Devon was on our calendar for a conference one day. "Devon, let's remember what your goals are." Devon had been working with this system for so long that he was able to clearly articulate his goals and tell us how

Figure 5.4 Reading Conference form with icons for Devon

Reading Conference with Icons

Strengths *Vocabulary* **Student** *Devon*

Goals and Strategies *Comprehension—Summarize text; include sequence of main events*
Expand Vocabulary—Tune in to interesting words and use new vocabulary . . .

Date / Touch Point	Observation and Instruction	Next Steps to Meet Goal
1-18 / Touch Point	*The Lightning Thief* *Oral summary* *Very long—shorten to most important*	*1. Read 2 chapters* *2. Summary for each chapter in journal* Next: *Meet in 2 days*
1-23 / Touch Point	*The Lightning Thief* *Review his summaries. Each were about 10 sentences long* *Together reviewed summary—cut out sentences to most important*	*1. Read 2 chapters* *2. Summarize in journal 3–6 sentences* Next: *Meet in 2 days*
1-27 / Touch Point	*The Lightning Thief* *Review summary—6 run on sentences* *Together whittle down to what is important*	*Read 4 chapters* *Write one summary* Next: *Meet 4 days*
Touch Point		Next
Touch Point		Next
Touch Point		Next

it was going. "I'm working on my comprehension by summarizing the story," he explained (see Figure 5.4).

"How is it going today? Can you read a bit of the story you are reading and do a quick summary?" Devon was able to read a paragraph or two, but we noticed that his summary had many details and was quite lengthy, and he was only halfway through the book.

"Devon, do you remember how we have been working together as a whole group on checking for understanding and writing those statements down as we read? Then we take those statements and turn them into our summary to help us remember the gist of what we've read? Your summary was a little too detailed and long. Let's try this. Get out your reader's notebook. Just like we did with the chapter book that we read aloud in class today, each time you stop to check for understanding, I want you to write the statement in your reader's notebook. It looks like you have four more chapters in this book. I'd like you to do that for the next two chapters. When you are done with those chapters, I want to meet with you again to go over those statements and show you how to keep the most important ones and move them into a paragraph. Then I'll have you do the same thing for the last chapters, and we'll meet again to show you how to do a whole book summary.

"So you have already read seven chapters; how long have you been reading this book?"

"I started it Monday."

"Since today is Thursday, it looks like you are reading about two chapters a day. That means you should be done with the next two by Monday. Does it sound reasonable if we meet Monday at one of the last rounds of Daily Five to go over your notes?"

Devon looked at us in his slow, easy manner and said, "I guess so."

Holding students accountable for reading is something we always keep in mind, which is why the goals and expectations we set for them are high.

Goal: Accuracy

Strategy: Cross Checking (Beginning Reader)

One of the first strategies we teach beginning readers is to use the pictures to support their reading. Haley, a very young five-year-old who knew a few letters and sounds, was reading a book about sack puppets. Each page showed a picture of a puppet with one word below the picture. When she came to the page that showed a turkey sack puppet, she stopped and looked at us, waiting to be told the word. What a great opportunity to teach this beginning reader to cross-check.

"Haley, look at the picture. Do you know what it is?"

"A bird," she said.

"Let's look at the letters in the word. The first letter in this word is a *t*. Do you know what sound *t* makes? That's right, it says /t/. Let's cross-check that letter and sound with the picture. Does the word *bird* start with the /t/ sound? It doesn't! So that word isn't *bird*. Can you think of a different word that would match the picture so it makes sense and then cross-check to see if it begins with a *t*?"

Haley quickly came up with the word *turkey*.

"Haley, look at you—you just used Cross Checking! You looked at the picture, looked at the first letter of the word, and made sure that what you were saying started with that letter and that it made sense! This is a great strategy for you right now. Haley, when you are reading during Daily Five, I want you to be sure and look at the pictures, then at the first letter of the words, just like you did in this book, and then see if you can figure out the word that would make sense. Do you remember what that strategy is called?"

Given her age, Haley had no idea that the strategy was called Cross Checking. So we reminded her. Often it takes many repetitions of hearing the strategy, having guided practice, and trying it out before they are able to label it.

We took a moment to record in our Pensieve under Haley's name the instruction we had just done with her and our plans for her next step, which was to keep this guided instruction going with this beginning reader. We set an appointment with Haley on the calendar in our Pensieve for the very next day. Our plan was to model Cross Checking again with her, have her practice with us, and then introduce the kinesthetic hand motions with the action as another way to anchor this all-important strategy in her brain.

Goal: Accuracy

Strategy: Cross Checking (Advanced Reader)

Once a student advances to reading books with chapters or text that are not always supported by pictures, the strategy of Cross Checking changes. While reading *Holes* by Louis Sachar, Colin read *exclaimed* instead of *excited*. Rather than stop him immediately, we waited until he came to the end of the sentence. He stopped, frowned a bit, and hesitated.

"What's wrong, Colin?"

"Well, that didn't make sense."

He then backed up and reread, a wonderful strategy, but he misread the word *excited* again. He frowned again. "It still doesn't make sense."

"Colin, let's use the Cross Checking strategy to see if you can figure out why what you are reading isn't making sense. This time when you read, I am going to ask you to slow way down. As you read each word, I want you to cross-check it by asking yourself, 'Does the word I am reading match the letters on the page, does it sound right, and does it make sense?'"

Colin backed up and began to reread. He noticed that when he read the word *excited* and instead said *exclaimed*, it didn't match the letters and it didn't make sense. He was then able to figure it out and move along. As Colin continued to read a bit more, he encountered the same problem. Colin is a wonderful reader who monitors for meaning while he reads. When given this advanced Cross Checking strategy, he was thrilled to have a way to help himself figure out a word that wasn't making sense as well as a plan of attack for fixing the problem.

"Colin, we worked on a new strategy today. Can you tell me what it is?"

"It's so great, 'cause it is Cross Checking just like I used to do when I was little, but now I don't use the pictures." Because of Colin's background with CAFE and the fact that he had been working with the strategies since kindergarten, he made the connection between advanced Cross Checking and the version he used "when he was little," a whopping three years ago!

"So Colin, when you are reading your book, I want you to be aware of when the story doesn't make sense to you. Then go back and reread like you always do, and give this new Cross Checking strategy a try to see if you can fix the problem. I'd like to meet with you in three days to check in and see how it is going."

In our Pensieve we recorded the book Colin was reading along with a note about the strategy we had worked on that day. We set an appointment with him on our calendar and jotted down our thinking about his next steps. After we met with him three days later, we decided to continue watching for data points as evidence of his use of strategy. Because Colin so easily made the transition from beginning cross checking to the more advanced version and saw immediate success with and value in the strategy, we didn't think he'd need sticky notes or his reader's response notebook to encourage practice. We would reevaluate this choice at his next conference.

Goal: Fluency

Strategy: Reread Text

Katie was a fourth grader reading at the third-grade level. Her reading was stilted and monotone from many years of reading books that were too difficult. She had practiced reading this way for so long that it was taking her twice as long as her classmates to read passages, and her comprehension was also affected. Fluency was her reading goal. She was a bright girl, and her sense of urgency to accelerate her reading was strong.

We met with Katie to begin the process.

"Katie, today we are going to learn a strategy that will help you become a more fluent reader. Remember last time we met we discovered that your reading pace is slow? You decided you want to read faster so you can read more books. Working on your fluency will help you accomplish this goal. You have also been choosing books that are too hard for you. If you are reading books that are a little easier for you, you will be able to practice reading faster and with more expression. Here is what fluent reading sounds like." We modeled reading a few lines accurately and smoothly with good expression.

"The strategy we are going to practice is Reread Text to make your reading smooth, accurate, and expressive. Rereading will give you a chance to practice your fluency. Here is how it is done. You will choose one paragraph from a story you are reading each day and reread that paragraph until you can read it smoothly and with expression. This shouldn't take more than five to eight minutes of your reading time each day, and it is practicing with only one paragraph a day. If you want, you can practice this Reread Text strategy during Read to Self or Partner Read, as well as at home. Let me show you what it looks and sounds like."

We read a paragraph slowly and choppily the first time to accentuate the errors and replicate her reading patterns. Then we reread the same paragraph three or four times, until we read it smoothly, accurately, and with expression.

"Katie, that is how you will practice the fluency strategy of rereading. It's your turn—give this a try."

Katie chose a paragraph and reread it three times, each time with more expression and confidence than the previous reading.

"Great, Katie! You chose a passage, you read it three different times, and each time you reread it, your reading became smoother and more expressive. This is exactly what you are going to do each day to improve your fluency. Here are some sticky notes. For the next few days in your reading, when you choose your passage to reread, put a sticky note by it. I am going to write your name down on my calendar for Friday—that's in three days—because I want to check in with you to see how this strategy is working." We opened up the Pensieve and wrote her name on Friday's date.

Goal: Expand Vocabulary

Strategy: Tune In to Interesting Words (Advanced Reader)

Checking our calendar, we noticed we had an appointment to meet with Ikman, a shy, very bright fifth-grade English language learner who could decode just about anything but struggled with comprehension. One of the reasons she had comprehension issues was her lagging English vocabulary. For Ikman's reading to progress, we needed to help her expand her vocabulary.

The last time we'd met with Ikman, we'd done her beginning-of-the-year assessments. Her strength was accuracy, because she could read the words correctly. She had two goals: comprehension and expanding her vocabulary. We decided to begin with expanding her vocabulary, as this area would help her the most with comprehension.

"Ikman, do you remember what your goals are for reading?" Ikman was reticent, and after waiting for her response, we repeated her goals for her.

"Ikman, would you read a bit of the book you are reading right now so I can listen in?" Ikman was reading a chapter book in which a farm was the setting. She was fascinated with farm life, but we suspected she had never been on a farm and was probably unfamiliar with many of the words. After she had read a couple of paragraphs, we asked her, "Ikman, are there any words in the part that you just read that you don't know the meaning of?"

Our first hurdle with children who are working on expanding their vocabulary is to be aware of the words whose meaning they don't know.

"This word *hay* doesn't make sense," she said. "Here it says, 'He took a nap in the hay.' But my brother always says 'Hey, Ikman,' so it doesn't make sense to me."

"You are correct, Ikman—the words sound the same but mean very different things! This word, *hay*, is actually a dry grass that farmers collect to feed to their cows and horses. Now go back and read the sentences around the word *hay* again and see if it makes sense to you."

Ikman read the sentence again, and her brown eyes sparkled with understanding. "I get it now, but wouldn't it be kind of itchy to lie in?" She really did understand the word!

"Now let's get out your personal word collector and add that word to the /h/ box and even draw a little picture to help you remember it."

We use a personal word collector (in the appendix) with most of our children. This simple sheet of paper is a smaller version of the poster-sized word collector we have hanging on our wall. Both word collectors are used to write down words that are new or words that students are trying to learn. The personal word collector is glued into the front of each student's reader's response notebook or binder. These words can also be used as part of Daily Five word work.

Even though the word *hay* was not a word Ikman would use a lot, she loved reading anything she could get her hands on about farms; so, for her, it was a good word to help with the goal of expanding her vocabulary and her strategy of Tune In to Interesting Words. We followed this same procedure with a couple more words from her reading so she had three new words on her word collector.

"Ikman, as you read, your goal is to continue practicing your vocabulary strategy of Tune In to Interesting Words. While you're reading, I want you to use these sticky notes and write down two or three words from your story that you find interesting and don't know the meaning of. Let me show you how to do this."

We proceeded to read a page of her book, wrote the word *silo* on a sticky note, and let the edge of the note stick out of the book to make it easy to find.

"See how I didn't know the word *silo* so I wrote it on the sticky note? This is what I want you to do today. Then tomorrow I'll meet with you again and go over the words to show you how to find out what they mean and see if they are words you want to add to your personal word collector.

"I also want you to get out your table-talk notebook and add at least one of these new words from your personal collector page or our class word collector so you can take it home and share it with your family tonight."

Table-talk notebooks are merely small notebooks that go back and forth from school to home. We love the 3-by-5-inch size with a spiral at the top. For students working on expanding vocabulary, a great strategy is to have them write down a word or two in their table-talk notebooks, along with a picture clue or a definition. They take their notebook home in the evening and share the new word and the definition, and use it in a sentence at the dinner table with their families. We have heard from many parents of our English language learners that they love the table-talk notebooks as a way of expanding their own vocabulary.

"Great work today, Ikman! I've put you down for tomorrow on the Pensieve calendar and will look over the words you have marked with sticky notes."

Chapter 6

Whole-Class Instruction

When we were younger teachers, our whole-class instruction was driven by a basal reader and the lessons included in the program. These were looonnnnggg lessons in which we imparted a lot of information to the entire class. Right after the lesson, students went to practice what we had taught, usually with a ditto or worksheet that was conveniently provided as part of the program package. The next day, we'd teach a different looonnnnggg lesson, and students again practiced the strategy or skill we'd yammered on about with another ditto or worksheet.

There were 135 different comprehension lessons we were expected to teach as part of the reading program package. Even though these were different strategies or skills, many looked similar. There were also more than 200 worksheets accompanying the lessons. Both felt staggering to us, and we began to research the workshop approach.

What a change over the years in how we work with the whole class! We embraced the move toward mini-lessons in literacy workshops over the past two decades, in part because they dovetail so well with what brain researchers say about the limited attention spans of students in whole-class instructional settings.

Now our whole-class instruction is brief and far more frequent. Instead of 135 comprehension strategies, we now teach a select few to the whole class from the CAFE Menu. Short bursts of instruction with practice in different texts over the full year has produced a more effective and successful program for our students.

With the old program, we'd finish one of the 135 lessons and never go back. Now we are never "finished" teaching a strategy. When we introduce a new strategy, we also refer to ones students have been exposed to in the past—reteaching, reinforcing, and helping students see new possibilities for how the strategies might help them as readers. We say things like, "Now that you're comfortable with the inferring strategy, let's look at how cross checking works with inferring to help you make sense of a text."

We've pared these strategies down to those that we find work consistently for our students, but we acknowledge that readers use other strategies in addition to the ones on our CAFE Menu. Teachers sometimes add to the menu beyond what we have here, based on their curriculum guides and knowledge of their students. Some of the strategies aren't taught at all in early primary grades, due to developmental appropriateness.

The structure of the Daily Five allows us to purposefully and effectively focus on the needs of our readers. The CAFE Menu helps us intentionally teach strategies that will help students achieve their goals.

In Chapter 3, we shared the first four strategies we consistently introduce to the whole class during the first day of school: Check for Understanding, Back Up and Reread, Tune In to Interesting Words, and Cross Checking. We always teach these during the first days of school, regardless of our students' age and experience—reinforcing, modeling, and getting the language of our work together imprinted in students' minds sets them up for success.

Following these lessons, our instruction becomes a mix of introducing new strategies, using our assessment data to provide what children need next, and revisiting and reteaching strategies we've already introduced. Many of our choices are governed by the age of the children we are working with.

The CAFE Instruction Sequence: It's Your Choice

"Is there a standard sequential order in which we teach the strategies?" is probably the most frequent question we hear from teachers who are just beginning to use the CAFE Menu. We've listed the strategies on the menu in roughly the order we introduce them in class, with strategies near the top of the lists usually introduced and used more frequently than the rest. The strategies near the bottom of the Comprehension column tend to be more sophisticated and usually are not introduced to primary students.

With the whole-group CAFE lessons, we are driven by our assessments, one-on-one conferring, and small-group observations. Our antennae are constantly on alert for skills and strategy needs that the majority of our students have in common so they can be addressed in the timeliest manner.

For example, last year when Joan was teaching kindergartners, many of her early whole-class lessons were on accuracy strategies, because her emergent students needed them the most. A number of her students were struggling with blends, so Blend Sounds was one of the first strategies she taught and reinforced repeatedly, even though it's placed fairly far down the Accuracy column of the menu.

These professional judgment calls come fairly easily to Joan because of her expertise with assessments and her experience with CAFE. New teachers who are trying to juggle assessment protocols, school standards, faculty expectations, student and family relationships, and a variety of academic lesson plans may feel too overwhelmed to select CAFE strategies based on emerging student needs. It is perfectly appropriate to follow the given sequence, alternating between columns to provide balance during the first months of school. As new teachers gain experience, they typically gain a sense of what needs to be retaught, how the strategies work together, and what instructional techniques work best with their students.

We are always trying to find that balance between following the leads of our students and making sure we move through the prescribed curriculum so that we've tackled every skill. As you match your curriculum to the CAFE Menu, you'll make adjustments and accommodations. Because of the structure of our workshops around Daily Five, with short periods built in for two or three whole-class lessons each day, we have no problem introducing or reinforcing as many CAFE strategies as we like throughout the year to the whole class.

In primary classrooms, we typically teach three whole-class strategy lessons a day. (Figure 6.1 shows a typical schedule.) These usually include one strategy each from the Comprehension and Accuracy columns, and one more from the Fluency or Expand Vocabulary column. We don't do as many fluency and vocabulary whole-class lessons, because they are so easily integrated into our whole-class read-alouds. Read-alouds provide a natural time to notice interesting words together or to demonstrate what it takes to read with expression and good pacing.

When we're introducing a strategy to the whole-group setting, we understand that some children aren't ready for it, so we don't expect them to go out and practice the strategy independently right after it is taught. Instead, we give children a bit of partner practice in the whole group, and send them on their way with an invitation to practice and an opportunity to share their strategy work with the group later.

Principles for Whole-Class Lessons

We'd like to walk you through a typical whole-class strategy lesson to show how it is added to the CAFE Menu and reinforced over time.

To introduce the accuracy strategy Flip the Sound, we gather students in the meeting area. This is a very basic, visual strategy that many novice readers find helpful.

If we are working with younger readers, we might begin this way: "Boys and girls, we've been talking a lot about accuracy strategies, which are strategies that help you read words. Today I've got a new

Figure 6.1 First-week schedule: primary and intermediate

Typical Literacy Block Schedule of First Week

Primary and Intermediate

8:50–9:00	Day begins, gather on rug, take attendance, opening poem
Literacy Block	
9:00–9:10	Whole-group strategy lesson, three ways to read a book
9:10–9:40	Launching Daily Five
9:40–9:45	Brain and body break—songs, poems, chants
9:45–10:00	CAFE Strategy Lesson One with a picture book
10:00–10:15	Brain and body break—songs, poems, chants
10:15–10:30	CAFE Strategy Lesson Two with a picture book
10:30–10:35	Brain and body break—songs, poems, chants
10:35–10:50	CAFE Strategy Lesson Three with a picture book
10:50–10:55	Brain and body break—songs, poems, chants
10:55–11:25	Shared writing/writer's workshop Introduction
11:25–11:30	Ready for lunch
11:30–12:10	Lunch and recess

Times are approximate.

strategy for you, and it's called Flip the Sound. The secret for success with this strategy is to know the different sounds letters make, and to listen until you hear a word that makes sense." Typically, when we introduce this accuracy strategy, we use chart paper instead of a picture book. We start with a word like *mad*, which is characteristic of the types of words that students make errors on. "Sometimes when you're reading, you might read this word as *made*, because that *a* can make two different sounds."

Right below the word *mad* on the chart, we write it in a sentence: "I got really mad when I lost my coat."

"Now let's look at this." We read, "'I got really made when I lost my coat.' Does that make sense? Let's go back to the word that doesn't sound right or make sense and try flipping the sounds." We make a flipping hand motion, starting with our palm up and then flipping it over. "Made . . . mad. Now let's back up and reread it. We're using the strategy we already know, Back Up and Reread. Now we've got to check for understanding—does it make sense? Hey, we know that strategy, too! So when we flip the sound, we also back up and reread and check for understanding to make sure we've flipped to the right sound. We flipped from *made* to *mad*."

"Let's do another one." We write another word, like *hop*. "Most of us know what this word says and means—it's the word *hop*. What's the other sound that vowel can make? Flip that right now. *Hop*, *hope*." Write *hope* in a sentence and read "'I really hop it's sunny tomorrow.' Turn to your partner and flip the sound of *hop*. What else could it be? Now let's read the sentence together: 'I really hope it is sunny tomorrow.' Does that make sense? Isn't Flip the Sound a great strategy? Let's put it up on our CAFE board."

We grabbed a blank strategy card. "Jaeger, would you write out the card for us during our next Daily Five period? You're going to write 'Flip the Sound.' I'm going to write the words on this sticky note so you can spell them correctly. If you could include a sketch of a picture to remind people of what that strategy is, that would be wonderful!"

"And Jaeger, remember to put your name on the card so people will know that if they need help remembering what the strategy is, they can come to you."

"Here's where we'll put the strategy card."

Jaeger writes a strategy card for the CAFE bulletin board.

Even with the yellow sticky note showing the correct spelling, we sometimes have to provide children with an extra card so they can redo their first try. We want this published work to be spelled correctly.

We review this strategy before students leave the gathering space by saying, "This is an accuracy strategy you can use all the time in your reading. Some of you might even try Flip the Sound today. If you do try the

The strategy card is added to the CAFE Menu.

A Big Book is useful for a whole-group strategy lesson.

strategy, you might want to share what you tried at the end of Daily Five during our sharing time." During the time at the end of our literacy workshop when we share and review strategies, we'll have Jaeger post Flip the Sound, and we'll ask anyone who tried Flip the Sound to model what they did for their classmates.

The next day, when it's time for a CAFE strategy lesson, we'll reinforce the new strategy. We grab a Big Book or put a book under the Elmo camera.

Prior to the lesson, we use sticky notes to bookmark good simple words for practicing flipping the sound. We begin with a review. "Remember, boys and girls, how we worked yesterday on the strategy of Flip the Sound? Jaeger made this card for our CAFE board." We direct attention to the card by physically touching it. "Remember how we practiced flipping the sound with a few words—*hop/hope* and *mad/made*?

"Let me show you again how to flip the sound." We get to one of the marked passages, read a word incorrectly, and then say, "Wait a minute—that didn't make sense."

The question "Did that make sense?" is significant when we introduce the Flip the Sound strategy. It's the language we want students to take with them in their heads when they are trying the strategy alone. Students try the strategy again with partners, providing gradual release in learning the strategy. We direct attention to the CAFE Menu by saying, "Let's remember what our accuracy strategies are." We read through the posted accuracy strategies on the CAFE Menu that we've added by that time in the year—Cross Checking and so on—so we're constantly reminding students that there are many strategies to use, and that not all of them will work in all situations. Then we send them out to practice again, reminding them that we'll be asking for volunteers at the end of Daily Five to share the strategies they've tried.

Whole-Class Lesson Elements

The Flip the Sound lesson follows a systematic progression of steps that we use whenever we introduce a new strategy. These brief, focused lessons follow this progression:

1. *We identify what is to be taught, and share the "secret to success" with the strategy.*
   In the CAFE Menu Ready Reference guide in the appendix, we list the "secret to success" for each of the strategies, as well as how the strategies are defined. Students love a secret, and that language alone helps them become full partners in their own learning. We tell them exactly what they need to do to succeed, and they are eager to give it a go.
2. *We teach the strategy.*
   The strategy has to be anchored to text in some way (picture book, chapter book, or chart paper), but the amount of text depends on the strategy being taught. We model, reinforce, or explain the strategy for one to five minutes. This instructional time is limited so students will have the energy and attention for the rest of the lesson components.
3. *Students practice with partners.*
   Students know who their partners are before the lessons begin. We spend a lot of time early in the year teaching children how to efficiently identify and work with partners, as well as the appropriate behaviors and what we expect during partner work. If procedures for working with partners are put in place during the first weeks of school, "turn and talk" during whole-group instruction becomes a

powerful tool for practicing and reinforcing any skill, and takes a minute or less.

While children practice with a partner, we listen and observe closely. We can get an immediate feel for whether or not children get it, if we need another round of teaching the strategy, or if we've goofed and taught something the students aren't ready for (or taught in a way that confused them).

4. *We select a student to write and illustrate the CAFE Menu strategy card (the first time it is taught).*
   We write the words on the sticky note so students will spell the words correctly (but even so, students like Jaeger may require a second attempt). We used to write the cards ourselves, but we've learned over time that the person who does the most work does the most learning. We learned a lot the year we wrote the cards—in beautiful handwriting with our carefully crafted illustrations. What we learned is that the students didn't actually see the cards when we did the writing. Students never used the cards or referred to them when they were all in our pretty handwriting. Now the words are in their handwriting, and they like looking at the pictures their classmates create to illustrate the strategies.

   We know lots of publishers want to offer premade strategy cards to save busy teachers time, and it's even tempting to run off sets of the CAFE strategy cards you create yourself for the whole school or grade-level teaching team. Resist! Resist! If you let students write and illustrate the cards, the learning is far more likely to stick.
5. *We review the strategy.*
   This wrap-up of the lesson anchors the strategy back to the CAFE Menu. We reiterate why we use the strategy and usually repeat specific reading situations when this strategy is most useful. To people outside of education, our work must seem enormously repetitive at times. But we think you can see from the conferring examples in the previous chapter that repetition is essential in learning; practices won't become routines without this continual repetition.
6. *We encourage practice during independent reading times.*
   We don't ask all children to practice at once during the independent work periods—we always reinforce that when they are ready to use the strategy, they can try it out. The invitation gives some students a purpose for their reading after the lesson. Knowing they might have a chance to share what they've tried is also an incentive for some students.

7. *We post the strategy after independent practice (the first time it is taught).*
   The posting happens during the sharing time at the end of our literacy workshop, often an hour or more after we have introduced the strategy. As Pressley notes, this is a visual aid that will help students remember the strategy and try it later (Block and Pressley 2002). Because the child who wrote the card posts it, we have another "teacher in the room" whom classmates will view as an expert on this strategy. We'll reinforce this in later days and weeks when we say, "Nakesia, why don't you partner-read with Jaeger since you're working on Flip the Sound and he's an expert on this strategy."
8. *We continually connect new strategies to strategies already on the CAFE Menu board.*
   We are always repeating the concept that CAFE is a menu, and that these strategies all work together. By making connections between new and previously introduced strategies on the board (especially those strategies of Back Up and Reread, Cross Checking, and Check for Understanding), students see how they work together, and how they need to be flexible as readers.

Sample Lessons

We'd like to share a few more lessons, to give a sense of the range of ways we present the CAFE strategies in quick, focused lessons.

Good-Fit Books Lesson

Goal: Fluency

Strategy: Read Appropriate-Level Texts That Are a Good Fit

Probably the most important lesson we teach young readers is the lesson on "good-fit books." We've documented the lesson in our Daily Five book and even published a short video of it (Boushey and Moser 2007). It is crucial for students to be able to self-select appropriate books for independent practice of the CAFE strategies.

This lesson introduces the goal of fluency, with the strategy of choosing books that are a good fit. We always have students, especially as we move up through the elementary grades, who equate being a strong reader with reading all the words expressively and well. We've been discouraged as we've seen more and more of these readers in the intermediate grades showing very little comprehension of what they are reading. In order for these readers to make the most of the CAFE Menu, they must be taught the criteria for selecting books. We developed the "good-fit books" lesson to help accomplish this.

We teach children about good-fit books through the analogy of shoes, so for this lesson, we come prepared with a bag of shoes. Inside our bag we have placed pairs of our "Sunday best" shoes, tennis shoes, snow boots, golf shoes, and our husbands' much-too-large shoes. We begin by pulling out each pair one at a time and asking our class what they think the purpose of these shoes would be. "Each pair of shoes has a purpose, sometimes obvious, sometimes not," we say. "But purpose is very important. We certainly would not wear snow boots to play golf!

"Just like choosing which shoes to wear for which activity, we always have a purpose when we choose a book. Whether it's to learn about a certain topic, continue with a beloved series, try a new genre, read something by a favorite author, or for a myriad of other reasons, the purpose is a key element in selecting a good-fit book."

The examination of shoes continues as we shift our discussion to the topic of interest. We guide students to see that we do not have soccer shoes, because we are not interested in playing soccer. However, we love to golf, play in the snow, and, as the well-worn tennis shoes convey, go for long walks. Conversations evolve from what shoes we would select to match our interests, to recognition that we select books based on personal interest as well.

We think it is important that interest not be overlooked when helping students learn to select books. Interest is crucial if we are going to get students to read the volume of materials necessary to move them from survival-level readers to lifelong readers who choose to read for information and pleasure. When we look at our own lives as readers, we realize that we seldom stick with books we are not interested in. Our motivation wanes, our minds wander, and we inevitably end up abandoning the text.

The last two things to consider when choosing a good-fit book are comprehending what we are reading and knowing most of the words. We go back to our bag of shoes, pull out our husbands' much-too-large shoes, put them on, and proceed to try moving around the room. Amid giggles and peals of laughter, the children readily and easily point out why our husbands' shoes are not a good fit. They are too big.

We then ask one of the kids if we can try on her tennis shoes. Another round of laughter; we can get them on our feet, but of course they are not a good fit—too small! Yes, these shoes meet our purpose and our interest, but they are clearly not a good fit. Just as shoes need to meet the needs for our purpose and interest, so must books. If we find a book that fits our purpose of gathering information for our report, and fulfills our interest, and is about our topic—rats—but we cannot read all the words or understand what we are reading, then just like our husbands' shoes, it is not a good fit.

We then have a few students whose feet are clearly a different size from a classmate's remove one shoe. We ask them to trade that shoe with another student who has a shoe that might fit their purpose and interest. When the traded shoes don't fit, we can talk once again about the shoes meeting their needs of purpose and interest but not fitting.

This dialogue is a yearlong anchor in our classroom to help children understand that just as our shoes must fit for us to be successful, so must the books we read fit our purpose and interest. Fluency strategies work hand in hand with the other CAFE strategies when purpose and interest are part of the process of choosing books.

Goal: Comprehension

Strategy: Infer and Support with Evidence

Inference is a tricky strategy for students of any age to understand. Often they can learn a definition for *inference*, but there is a big gap between defining the term (or even understanding it) and being able to put it to use while reading. This lesson helps students bridge that gap.

We begin with "Today I want to show you how we infer throughout the day, not just while reading. We are going to play a game I call the Inferring Game. We are going to play this often, and you can even play it at home. We are going to read some statements that have clues about what is happening, but with some important information left out. We are going to be detectives to see if we can figure out the meaning behind the statement. Sometimes people even call this reading between the lines. I will read a statement and show you how to play."

We read aloud, "'You are in school sitting at your desk when all of a sudden you hear this ear-piercing noise and everyone gets up and walks out of the class.'

"The purpose of this game is to take all the clues and try to figure out what is happening in the statement. We are going to write the clues that are helping us understand what is happening on the board. Let's see, *school, piercing noise, everyone walks out.* Now we'll use our prior knowledge and think about all these words together . . . I think it is a fire drill. Do you agree? Why?

"Now let's have you try it. You are going to work with your elbow buddies and take turns so everyone will get a chance to play the Inferring Game. First, decide the order of who will go first and who will go second. Turn to your buddy and make that decision now. Show me with your fingers who is one"—hands go up—"and who is two"—the rest of the hands go up.

"Okay, number twos, you are first. When I say a statement, you will lean in and tell your elbow buddy your clues and then tell them what you think is happening. We will then switch and number ones will tell number two their clues and their thinking. Ready? Here is the first one."

We read each of the following statements, allowing for think time, buddy talk, and class discussion. At the end of the lesson, we review the secret to understanding and using this strategy.

The Inferring Game

Your mom came home with a bag from the Nintendo store.
You hear a truck in your neighborhood that is playing sweet music on a very hot day.
Your dad stomps into the living room, turns off the TV, and frowns at you.
The baseball game is on and you hear loud cheering.

Students love playing this game. We start with a few statements and then ask them to keep their eyes and ears open to the inferences they are making each and every day. We ask them to write these down, and each day students share the inferences they noticed. It also provides some great writing opportunities throughout the day. This game paves the way for helping children understand the concept of inferring when they read. We play it often, all year long.

Goal: Comprehension

Strategy: Summarize Text; Include Sequence of Main Events

This lesson is an example of how we integrate instruction into a read-aloud, especially in the intermediate grades. As we are reading aloud to our students, we tell them, "Today, girls and boys, we are going to work on summarizing. Summarizing is taking larger selections of text and reducing them to their bare essentials: the gist, the key ideas, the main points that are worth noting and remembering . . . I am going to read this picture book to you, and at the end we are going to summarize what happened. Remember, while we are reading, we are thinking and checking for understanding because we are going to take all the big thoughts of checking for understanding and collapse them down into the most important ideas of the story. That will give us the gist of the book so we can remember what it is about. Today each time we stop and check for understanding we are going to write key phrases of that thought on our chart. When the story is finished, we will look at all those ideas, pick the most important ones, and combine them into a summary."

As we read the story, we stop six times to check for understanding. Each time we stop, we write the synopsis of the section we just read and record it on the chart paper. At the end of the story, we have six statements about the book.

"Girls and boys, we have six phrases on the chart from when we stopped to check for understanding. Each phrase is a short summary of what was happening at that time in the book. We are going to reread these phrases, be certain they are all necessary, and then combine them into one paragraph."

We model rereading and thinking aloud through each of the phrases to be sure they include only the big ideas from the reading. Then, in front of them, we eliminate any unnecessary pieces because they give too much detail. We rewrite the phrases into a short paragraph.

"Now let's reread the paragraph. Does it give us the gist of the whole story? Is it in order? This is an example of how we summarize a story."

We model this process, connecting it to check for understanding each time we read aloud for an entire week. When we notice that some of the children are grasping the idea, we have them begin making and writing the Check for Understanding phrases. We model and work together more and more on this process of summarizing, little by little giving over the responsibility to our children. This strategy is one we work on all year long.

Goal: Expand Vocabulary

Strategy: Tune In to Interesting Words

Building an awareness of words is infused throughout our teaching day. It can be very easy and enjoyable to teach to students, because we are conveying a sense of wonder and delight over the unique and descriptive words authors add to their writing. This pleasure in words quickly transfers to students, and they readily begin noticing interesting words on their own. At times we must be good actors to get the point across. During our read-aloud, we periodically stop and focus on a word. It often sounds something like this:

"'The rain came down in a *deluge*, making it difficult to breathe or see.'

"Girls and boys, listen to this word we just read, *deluge*. We sure love to say the word, but what do you think it means? Let's reread the sentences around it and see if we can decide what the meaning of the word is." We reread a few sentences before and after the word. "Any ideas?"

We add to our word collector all year long.

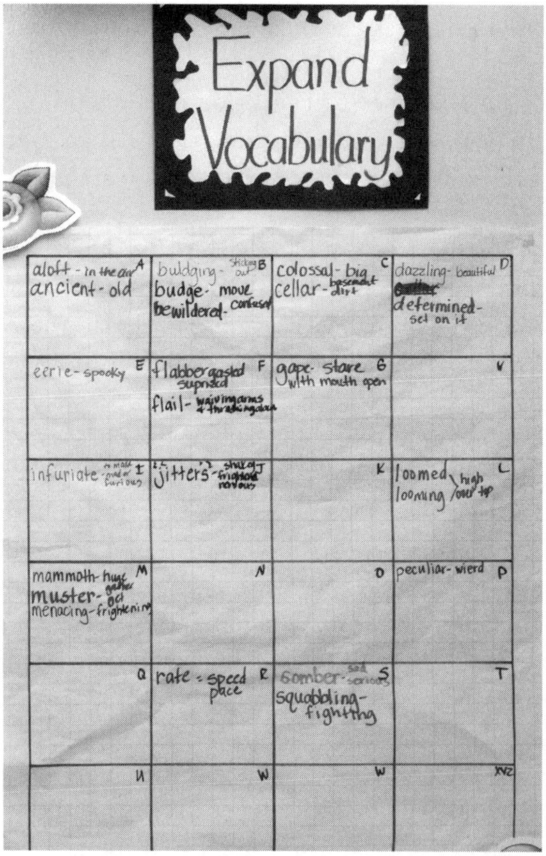

Hands are raised, some tentatively, some with exuberance. "I think it means 'on the ocean,'" Brinder says.

"No, I think it is talking about how the rain comes down," replies Nadeshda.

"My grandma always says it's raining cats and dogs," says Carson, "and I think it means 'raining very hard,' because it also says they couldn't see."

"Let's see if that makes sense. 'It was raining so hard it was difficult to breathe or see.' Does that fit? It sure does, and that is what deluge means, 'a drenching rain.' Have any of you ever been out in a drenching rain? Living here in Seattle, we could use that word a lot. We love that word! It's a wonderful way to describe how hard it is raining in the story. Let's go ahead and add it to our word collector." Our word collector is a compilation of the words we've discovered as a class. They are arranged in alphabetical order on the wall we've given over to language work.

In front of the class, either one of our students or we add the word to our word collector poster under the letter *D*. We always add a short definition of the word, or, for younger students and English language learners, a picture. "Who thinks you will be able to challenge yourself to use the word *deluge* either in your writing or at home with your parents by tomorrow?"

Molly is waving her hand in the air. "I can't wait to go home tonight and tell my mom that Kamara and I were playing on the big toy at recess and we were in a deluge!"

"Turn to your elbow buddy. Each of you use the word *deluge* as if you were talking to someone at home or in a piece of writing." We always try to have kids begin to use the word orally right from the start. We often review other posted words by asking kids to turn and talk to an elbow buddy and use one of the words off the word collector. This is a wonderful thirty-second strategy to use when they are in line for lunch or recess.

Selecting stories written with rich language makes it much easier to find (and tune in to) wonderful words. By focusing on three of four words a day, our students quickly become aware that tuning in to interesting words is fun. We love that it isn't intimidating like the workbook pages and flash cards of our past. (See the following list for some of our favorite books to read for vocabulary development.)

Some Favorite Titles for Building Vocabulary

You might consider a few of these titles if you are looking to add to your book repertoire. They are some of our favorites for tuning into interesting words and building vocabulary.

Title	Author
Clever Ali	Nancy Farmer
Flossie & the Fox	Patricia C. McKissack
*The Harmonica***	Tony Johnston
Lilly's Purple Plastic Purse	Kevin Henkes
*Little Green**	Keith Baker
Mr. George Baker	Amy Hest
My Father's Hands	Joanne Ryder
My Rows and Piles of Coins	Tololwa M. Mollel
Pebble; A Story About Belonging	Susan Milord
Skippyjon Jones	Judy Schachner
Some Birthday!	Patricia Polacco
Thundercake	Patricia Polacco
Very Hairy Bear	Alice Schertle
Wolf	Becky Bloom

**Short, fairly simple text. **Content makes it more suitable for intermediate students.*

Typically once or twice a week we even find ourselves bringing in a newspaper or magazine article with an interesting or wonderful word to share. Showing children that we pay attention to interesting words outside of school also helps them with their vocabulary development beyond the walls of our classroom.

As a class we may decide to put the word brought from home on our class word collector or we may not. Many a heated discussion has been had over words brought from home by a student or teacher as the class tried to decide if a word was worthy enough to go on our class word collector. It is always amusing to hear our students gently tell us that although the word we brought in was interesting, perhaps we could put it on our personal word collector instead of the class word collector.

As you've seen in the preceding examples, building the CAFE Menu can easily be integrated into whole-class strategy lessons you have likely used successfully for years to teach reading and vocabulary, to create word walls, or to focus your read-aloud. There is nothing particularly unique about the sample lessons we've shared. Our goal is to help you see that CAFE isn't "one more thing" you have to somehow find time to teach. Lessons you have taught successfully for years likely fall into one of the four category headings and can easily be integrated. It is simply a visual organizational tool that can help you link assessment data and goal setting into purposeful, intentional instruction.

In the next chapter, we show how CAFE helps us organize and think through small-group instruction.

Chapter 7

Strategy Groups

A few years back, Joan was in a rut with her hairstyle. Each day, after emerging from the shower, the laborious process of getting her hair ready for the world was torture. Joan had been going to the same hairdresser for years and liked her very much. The relationship was comfortable, and the outcome was predictable. However, each day saw Joan blowing and rolling, teasing and tugging—the ritual demanded more time than she really wanted to spend to become presentable.

After one particularly bad hair day, Joan ran into her friend Marie. The first thing she noticed was Marie's great haircut. Joan learned that not only was the coveted haircut darling, but it took less than five minutes to fix. *Hmm*, Joan thought, *maybe if I found a new hairdresser, the outcome would be much better*. However, the process of changing was certain to be challenging and maybe even painful. Yet seeing her friend's hairstyle made Joan realize that perhaps something better was out there.

Joan left Marie with her hairdresser's number in hand. A few weeks later found Joan sitting in the chair of Tracy, the new hairdresser. She explained how unhappy she was with how much time her hair was taking each day, and how it had become so brittle from coloring that it felt like straw. Tracy jumped right in, and not being one to mince words, let Joan know that not only was the cut wrong for her face, but that her hair was in poor health. Drastic measures were called for: he would cut it short and take her back to her regular color. Joan had been coloring her hair for so long that she wondered what her "regular" color was.

She will never forget the anticipation of sitting in the chair while the towel was removed from her wet head. There was an audible gasp from Tracy and the other patrons in the salon. Joan's new short cut was now an indescribable shade of Day-Glo orange! All the products and practices of the past had damaged Joan's hair at a much deeper level than Tracy had realized.

Six hours later and with a much lighter wallet, Joan emerged from the hairdresser with a wonderful new look. So what does Day-Glo-orange hair have to do with strategy groups? For many years our reading instruction was limited to whole-group instruction or what we think of now as the "spray and pray" method. Our small groups were leveled and never flexible. We had the Red Bird group, the Blue Bird group, and, of course, the Buzzards, who would remain Buzzards all year long. (We jest, of course, regarding the Buzzards, but it isn't too far from the truth.)

As our careers progressed, we moved to small "guided reading" group instruction. We soon realized our small-group instruction had merely transferred the "spray and pray" methods to smaller fields. Yes, we had only four to six kids in these small guided groups, and yes, they were grouped by ability level, which helped make gathering materials easier. But within that group, we still had one or two students who needed comprehension help, one or two who needed more support decoding the text, and one who might need work with fluency and vocabulary. All these children were technically reading at the same level, but in reality, their needs were very different.

As we became more proficient at assessing students and identifying their needs as readers, our beliefs began to shift regarding small-group instruction. Why not start grouping kids together by strategy need rather than reading level? If our goal for small-group instruction was to help children read and comprehend any text, we wanted to make our small-group time more focused on each child's needs. It seemed most logical to have children with the same needs grouped together to receive their instruction, regardless of reading level.

This shift in thinking about strategy-group instruction was much like the disequilibrium Joan found with her hair crisis. She was comfortable doing what she had been doing for years: going to the same hairdresser and sticking with the same cut and color, even when that routine was taking more and more time and her hair was becoming more and more unhealthy. We knew our guided reading groups were taking a lot of time and really weren't meeting our students' needs. But the leap into the unknown of a new way scared us away from making big changes for years.

Since moving from guided reading groups to strategy groups was a huge shift in thinking for us, it's no surprise that this is the part of the CAFE program many teachers find the most challenging. Keep in mind that we didn't shift all of our leveled groups to flexible groups overnight. It has been a change in our thinking over time as we've worked with children, read the research, and strived to match our teaching to the needs of our students.

Grouping Through the Years

We've both taught for more than twenty-five years, so we've seen many changes in the field when it comes to grouping. When we first started teaching, we had a basal with one anthology for all of our kids, and we taught everything in reading with whole groups. Whole-group instruction and corresponding workbook pages were the sum total of our reading program. We knew enough to know it wasn't working, but we were young, without the confidence or experience to make changes on our own. We changed only when our schools presented us with a new, "improved" program.

The next phase was a new basal with an anthology, which included class sets of trade books coupled with a few days of whole-group instruction. From there we began to be able to allow students more choices. A few students might be reading chapter books or stories of their choice some of the time during our reading program. We'd instruct with the basal for a few weeks, then chapter books with the whole class for a few weeks, and then go back to the basal. By the 1980s, we felt like we had permission to be a little creative and mix it up. There was room for themes and fun response activities, but not a clear sense of what was expected of us—and so we didn't convey a clear sense to our students.

It was at this point in our careers that we began to feel most frustrated, because we were learning enough about the reading process to know we really weren't meeting the needs of our students. We'd gone to graduate school for our master's degrees and had begun to look more closely at our students as individuals. Our most capable students thrived, simply because they could thrive in any environment. But we weren't seeing progress with our most needy learners. And we didn't have good assessments to help us figure out what was going on, or how our teaching might change.

We thought students were growing as readers (in some situations in our classrooms), but we weren't really sure. By the time the 1990s rolled around, we started to get training in guided reading. We had better assessments, and we could determine a level for each child. We had freedom to use the basal or any leveled books in these groups, and put together groups of students for instruction based on their levels.

"Doing guided reading" was the focus of our reading instruction for quite a few years. What we eventually realized is that any given group of students reading at Level 5 or Level 22 still contained students with very different needs. Some within a group had strong fluency but could understand almost nothing they read. Other students in the same group read painfully slow but comprehended everything they read. We still weren't meeting the different needs of these students who were put together by levels alone.

About that time, we started hearing research that said our groups needed to be "flexible." But what did that mean? How flexible could our groups be, if the sole criterion for placing children in groups was their reading level?

This is when we started to develop strategy groups as an alternative to guided reading, because we needed a system for grouping students around something other than reading levels that would meet their needs. The Strategy Groups assessment form in our Pensieves gave us a way to cluster students with the same need, even though at times these students were reading at very different levels. At other times, students with the same need were reading at the same level, but levels were no longer our sole criterion for grouping.

We hope you realize that we didn't suddenly have an epiphany and switch all our groups from leveled guided reading to strategy groups. Instead, we began with one strategy group, testing the idea within the whole class, which still had guided reading as the main model for small groups.

Our first strategy group was an accuracy group working on the skill Chunk Letters and Sounds Together. These children were emergent readers, and it was easy to pull them away from the rest of the class during our reading workshop. The other students could readily read and work silently while we were with this group.

The shift to the strategy groups made us rethink our management of small groups in many ways. At that point in our teaching, we'd developed the Daily Five and the CAFE Menu, but the calendar for individual conferences and small groups wasn't yet part of our Pensieve. We quickly realized we would never be able to keep track of strategy groups without a calendar to note our meetings with individual students and strategy groups. The guided reading groups weren't meeting our students' needs fully, but at least it was easy to meet with three or four groups a day during reading workshop, and these groups rarely shifted much during the year. We'd meet with the red and blue groups one day, and the yellow and green groups the next day. There was no variation in the schedule for guided reading, and it was easy for everyone to remember.

Once we moved to strategy groups, students were moved in and out of groups all the time—sometimes with students of similar levels, sometimes grouped with classmates who read at different levels.

The strategy being addressed in the group also affected the frequency with which the groups would get together. Some strategy groups met for just a couple of days; others continued for two weeks or more, depending on how sophisticated the strategy was and how well the children were mastering it.

Do we still have groups of students working at the same level in these strategy groups? Of course, especially with emergent readers, who have many needs. But even then, their reading level is not the reason they were grouped together; it just happens that these young readers are often at similar beginning reading levels.

Many of our intermediate readers also participate in literature circles and book clubs in three- to four-week cycles. They may also meet with their teacher in strategy groups, and all participate in one-on-one conferring. As students move up through the elementary grades, the differences in their needs can become more and more pronounced. In these situations, one-on-one conferring is more essential than strategy-group work, because individual conferences are the best way to target their needs.

Structuring and Managing Strategy Groups

We've already given many examples in Chapter 6 of how we gather notes for putting together strategy groups as we confer with individual students. We do not pull strategy groups early in the year until a couple of things have happened. First, we assess and confer with every student so that we know what his and her goals and strategy needs are. Second, we need to have Daily Five up and running smoothly in our classrooms so that we are confident all students will be able to work independently when we meet with groups. Typically, the assessments, first conferences, and implementation of Daily Five take four to six weeks. We will likely have our first strategy-group meetings in early to mid-October, since school for us starts the first week of September.

A lot of instruction is still taking place during this first four to six weeks of school, since we are doing daily instruction of the whole-group CAFE Menu strategies (see Chapter 6 for more examples of whole-class instruction) and individual conferences with students (see Chapter 5 for more examples of conferring). Even after strategy groups are in place, much of our instruction continues to take place in whole-class and individual conference settings.

Using the Strategy Groups Form

Generally, at the end of four to six weeks, everyone has been assessed, we've conferred with everyone, Daily Five is up and running—and we are ready to form strategy groups. You'll see on the sample Strategy Groups form (Figure 7.1) that we've clustered students based on needs, but the bulk of the sheet remains empty for planning for the groups.

To launch a strategy group, we ask students to come to the meeting area with their book boxes. We normally start with a group of students who are

Figure 7.1 Sample Strategy Groups form

Strategy Groups and Instruction

Goal Comprehension	Strategy Check for Understanding	Names	Touch Points
Date	Lesson	Sevilya Inna Sandy Juan	

Goal Accuracy	Strategy Flip the Sounds	Names	Touch Points
Date	Lesson	Jaeger Amanda Josh Haley Colin	

Goal Vocabulary	Strategy Tune In to Interesting Words	Names	Touch Points
Date	Lesson	Brandon Ikman Samuel Sandy	

most at risk. They take out a text they are using for individual reading and begin quietly reading aloud. We listen in, just like in individual conferences, to see whether they are using the strategy we're going to tackle (see Figure 7.2). After thirty to sixty seconds of listening to their reading, we stop them and reinforce the group's goal. We might say, "You're all working individually on the strategy of Back Up and Reread." If it's the first day of a small

Figure 7.2
Coaching Toward a Target

Coaching Toward a Target: Small Group

Productive, Effective, Focused Teaching and Learning

1. Check calendar for appointments.
2. Prepare (30 seconds)
   Review your notes for last meeting.
3. Observe (1–2 minutes) *"[Student], please get out a book and read so I can listen in; then tell me about yourself as a reader."*
   Observe the student. Is he or she applying the skill/strategy taught or reinforced last time you met?
   What is the student doing well with his or her strategy/skill application?
   Record this on the conferring sheet.
4. Reinforce and Teach (2–4 minutes)
   "I noticed ________; what did you notice? Today we are going to ________."
   Verbally share with student your observations of what he or she was doing well.
   Teach or reinforce the skill or strategy you feel is just right for the student now by
   - explicit explanation,
   - modeling,
   - thinking aloud,
   - offering advice.
5. Practice (2–3 minutes) *"Now it is your turn. You try . . . "*
   Ask the student to practice the skill/strategy while you listen in.
6. Plan (30 seconds) *"This is what I am hearing, and because of that, this may be our next step."*
   Based on today's teaching and learning, decide and agree together what the next step will be. It isn't uncommon for students to need continued practice with the previous strategy.
   Write this plan on the Strategy Groups form.
7. Encourage (15 seconds)
   Just before you leave the student, encourage him or her to continue to practice the skill taught or reinforced today.
   Student should articulate the goal.

- The times above serve as guidelines, and though it isn't necessary to strictly adhere to them, they will give you a general idea so you can keep your conferences focused and brief.
- Each step above may be shorter or longer, depending on what the students are doing that day, and where you are in the gradual release of teaching the skills or strategies to the students.
- Remember that brief, focused conferences that occur frequently are considerably more beneficial than sporadic, lengthy ones.

group, we always model. We say, "Let's show you what that looks like with this text we are reading." We place a text on the floor in front of them, so they can practice with us if they choose. We model for a minute or two, and then students practice with their independent books while we listen in and coach. We then reinforce the target for the group: "What's your goal? What's the strategy you are working on?" This is when we decide whether

Strategy Groups and Instruction

Goal Fluency **Strategy** Reread Text

Date	Lesson	Names	Touch Points
1-17	Model—Shel Silverstein poem—Practice as a group	Katie	3
1-19	Review poem—Review strategy—practice		
1-23	Check group for good-fit books—students share reading their own stories.	Colin	4
1-25	Bring in poetry books, each choose and practice	Zach	3, 3
1-29	Partner Read and practice		
1-31	Most are getting this—make sure they have good-fit books	Josh	4, 4, 4
2-2	Students state their purpose for using this strategy		

Goal Accuracy **Strategy** Use Beginning and Ending Sounds

Date	Lesson	Names	Touch Points
1-15	Use Jack and Jill Nursery Rhyme—recite rhyme together—frame the word j-a-c-k. Look at beginning and ending sounds, do the same with Jill.	Nadjae	
		Haley	
1-16	Review beginning and ending sounds. Review Jack & Jill. Point and choose hill to frame and stretch each sound. Use leveled books with 1 sentence on each page—read and frame.	Colin	
1-17	Use Humpty Dumpty—recite poem—frame 2 words read together focusing on beginning and ending sounds. Review books from yesterday. Choral read. Choose 2 words to focus on beg. and end.	Donita	

Goal Vocabulary **Strategy** Tune In to Interesting Words 2/7 add—Use prior knowledge . . .

Date	Lesson	Names	Touch Points
1-10	Introduce word collectors—purpose—how to use Add 2 words a day from their reading	Brandon	
1-17	Review word collectors—what do your words mean—how do you figure out the meaning	Ikman	
1-24	May need to add Use prior knowledge and context to predict and confirm meaning—review each word collector	Samuel	
2-7	Started layering on Use prior knowledge	Sandy	

Strategy Groups and Instruction

Goal Comprehension **Strategy** Check for Understanding

Date	Lesson	Names	Touch Points
1-10	Bring read-aloud to group—Model from today's readings, all practice	Sevilya	
1-11	Each practice in own book	Inna	3
1-12	I will call on each one during read-aloud to practice—How did it go?	Sandy	3, 4, 4
1-16	When do you use this strategy? Each share with group—give examples in own story	Juan	3
1-18	Partner group—practice with own stories with other person checking for understanding		

Goal Accuracy **Strategy** Flip the Sounds

Date	Lesson	Names	Touch Points
1-10	Whiteboard—Review long and short "a"—practice flipping	Jaeger	
1-11	Whiteboard—Review flipping sounds with "a"		
1-12	Whiteboard—Review long and short "i"—flip "i" and "a" words	Amanda	4, 4, 4
1-15	Whiteboard—Review "a" and "i" sounds find in own books		
1-16	Whiteboard—Review "o" sounds—flip each	Josh	
1-17	Whiteboard—Review a, i, o—flip and find in own books		
1-18	" —Review "e" sounds—flip each—practice	Haley	
1-19	" —Review a, e, i, o flip and find in books		
		Colin	3, 4

Goal Comprehension **Strategy** Summarize Text; Include Sequence of Main Events

Date	Lesson	Names	Touch Points
1-12	Define summary—model one verbally using the class read-aloud	Devon	
1-18	Sandy joined—review summarize, students share their own interpretation. I write in front of the group a summary from our read-aloud. Adding critical elements.	Brandon	
1-24	Partnered—each child tells the other a summary of their own book so far—in 4–5 sentences. Listen for main elements—Repeat back. Student writes summary from their own story—bring it back next time.	Simon	
		Sandy	

Figure 7.3 Sample Strategy Groups form

they can leave to practice on their own or whether they need to work with a partner. We also plan when we are going to meet next. Depending on the group, we might meet the next day, or we might choose to have some days of individual conferring between meetings.

The structure and format of these groups is very similar to individual conferences. What we gain through strategy-group meetings is twofold: we save time, and we build our reading community. We can sit on the floor, use a shared text, and model for students, having students try the strategy simultaneously. This way we can reach four or five children at the same time, rather than having to teach the same skills repeatedly to individuals.

Our strategy groups help us use our instructional time most efficiently and are a way to partner students who are working on the same strategy so that they can help and support one another. We can create buddy systems and provide that extra piece of buddy support for needier students through the small strategy groups. It's also a chance for students to double-dip—to hear the strategy in small groups as well as individual conferences.

In Figure 7.3, you'll see the strategy groups from January in Joan's primary classroom. Notice that Brandon, a student reading on a fourth-grade level, was in two different groups during this period, one on comprehension

(Summarize Text) and one on expanding vocabulary (Tune In to Interesting Words). Donita, reading at a pre-primer level, was in the accuracy—Use Beginning and Ending Sounds group, all of whose members were emergent readers working on beginning and ending sounds for six weeks. Sandy was in three different groups: comprehension (Summarize Text), accuracy (Check for Understanding), and expand vocabulary (Tune In to Interesting Words). After mastering the strategy Check for Understanding in her first group, she was moved to the Summarize Text group.

You might think from looking at this chart that Joan had a small class because there are only twenty-one student names here. But three students weren't in strategy groups during this period. Their needs were being met in one-on-one conferences.

The forms get very messy as students move in and out of groups. When a student has mastered a strategy, we draw a line through the student's name. If a flexible group is already working on that student's next strategy, we add him or her to that group. If he or she is working on a skill that we don't have a group for, we keep an eye out for students who might work on that strategy and become part of a new flexible group, and we start a new box on the form. In the meantime, we meet the student's needs one on one.

This is the power of flexible strategy groups that use shared short texts or individual book-box books: students can join groups at any time, and groups can be reformed or disbanded as needed. In previous years, we were sometimes forced to juggle too many guided reading groups because students were at such different levels. Or a child would make rapid progress, and we'd have to figure out a way to integrate him or her into a group where students were already halfway through a shared text.

We always faced management issues with leveled groups because of shortages of materials. We often had a hard time finding enough copies of shared texts at a particular level, and were frantically scrounging for books in the school leveled book room or borrowing from colleagues in the morning and returning the books in the afternoon so they could have them for their teaching. It wasn't ideal.

Strategy Groups in Action: What a Typical Morning Looks Like

After we go through morning routines, we typically start the literacy block with a whole-class read-aloud and strategy lesson from the CAFE Menu. After the lesson, we call the names of students who will be meeting with us

Figure 7.4
Primary schedule for weeks 6+

Typical Literacy Block Schedule Weeks 6+

or After Daily Five or Literacy Routines Are in Place

Primary

8:50–9:00	Day begins, gather on rug, take attendance, opening poem
Literacy Block	
9:00–9:15	CAFE Strategy Lesson—Comprehension with a picture book
9:15–9:35	Round One of Daily Five—Teacher works with small group, then confers with three to four students
9:35–9:45	CAFE Strategy Lesson—Accuracy
9:45–10:05	Round Two of Daily Five—Teacher works with small group, then confers with three to four students
10:05–10:15	CAFE Strategy Lesson—Fluency/Expand Vocabulary
10:15–10:35	Round Three of Daily Five—Teacher works with small group, then confers with three to four students
10:35–10:45	Share/review of strategies
10:45–11:25	Shared writing/writer's workshop
11:25–11:30	Ready for lunch
11:30–12:10	Lunch and recess

Times are approximate and vary.

for the first strategy group of the day, and then we do a check-in for Daily Five so that the other students are set for independent work (see Figures 7.4 and 7.5 for examples of typical schedules).

Students who are in the first strategy group get their book boxes and join us on the rug. The rule of thumb we use for how long the groups run is based on the age of the students. The approximate age of the students is the approximate number of minutes they can sustain higher-level thinking with group instruction. If we are working with a group of seven-year-olds, our strategy group will be approximately seven minutes long. If we are working with twelve-year-olds, we can go for ten to fifteen minutes.

Once the group lesson is completed, we release them with a job to do (to practice the strategy by themselves or with a partner in the group). We get up and grab our Pensieve, and for the remainder of the round of Daily Five, we do three or four one-on-one conferences with students. The next

Figure 7.5
Intermediate schedule for weeks 6+

Typical Literacy Block Schedule Weeks 6+

or After Daily Five or Literacy Routines Are in Place
Intermediate

8:50–9:00	Day begins, gather on rug, take attendance, opening poem
Literacy Block	
9:00–9:25	CAFE Strategy Lesson—Comprehension with a picture book
9:25–10:10	Round One of Daily Five—Teacher works with small group, then confers with five to eight students
10:10–10:35	Strategy Lesson—Writing
10:35–11:15	Round Two of Daily Five—Teacher works with small group, then confers with five to eight students
11:15–11:30	Share/review strategies
11:30–12:10	Lunch and recess

Times are approximate and vary.

round of Daily Five begins in about twenty to thirty minutes (depending on the time of year and students' stamina). We do another whole-class lesson, then call together another strategy group, send the rest of the class off for independent work after check-in, conduct the strategy group, then use the time after the strategy group for more conferences.

In primary classrooms, we typically have time for three rounds of Daily Five each morning. Intermediate classes usually have time for two.

Strategy groups are a truly flexible format. In the remainder of this chapter, we share three examples of the different instruction that goes on in these groups, linked to the goals and strategies the groups are working on.

Sample Strategy Groups

Goal: Accuracy

Strategy: Use Beginning and Ending Sounds (Kindergartners)

The group of five-year-olds has gathered on the green oval rug in the corner of Joan's room, in front of a handwritten chart of a common nursery

We use a variety of materials with our strategy groups.

rhyme, "Jack and Jill." This group of students knows the majority of their letters, and they have begun to attempt reading everything they see. It is a very exciting time for these children; everything about kindergarten seems to excite them. Joan has noticed—during whole-class choral reading and on preliminary assessments—that they look at the first letter and the vowel, then put them together and make a guess at the word.

"Girls and boys, look at what I brought for us to read today. Remember when I read with each one of you and we set your goals—remember what we are going to work on to help you become really smart readers? The great thing is that you all have the exact same goal, accuracy, which means 'to be able to read the words correctly.' The strategy we are going to work on is Use Beginning and Ending Sounds to help you read accurately."

Joan points to the chart paper. "This is a nursery rhyme. Do any of you know any nursery rhymes?" A few of the kids know some nursery rhymes and began to say them with enthusiasm. "We are going to read this one together. I'm going to start by showing you the accuracy strategy Use Beginning and Ending Sounds to read the title of this poem. Let's see, this first word starts with a *J*. I know that the letter *J* says /j/. The next letter is *a* and a says /a/." Because these are emergent readers, most of them know the short-vowel sounds; however, the long vowels are still a work in progress. This particular rhyme contains mostly short vowel sounds, so it is a good choice for the group.

"Hmm, let me look at the end of the word. It ends with a *k*, and I know that *k* says /k/. I have to be sure to pay attention to the end of the word so I read it correctly. Let's see, I am going to use another accuracy strategy to help me blend these sounds together." Even though *Blend Sounds Together* is not their immediate goal and she has not talked to this group about this strategy, Joan casually adds this phrase to the conversation. She constantly models that readers use more than one strategy at a time to read. Most of this group won't pick up on the fact that she has dropped a second strategy into the mix, but labeling what we do for kids as we do it will help build background that will come in handy later on.

"So let's look, /j/, /a/, /ck/. When I blend that together, I think it says *Jaaack*, *Jack*!" Nadjae, a high-energy little girl who knows some nursery rhymes, can't help but bounce up on her knees and say, "Jack! I bet this one is Jack and Jill went up the hill!" We never worry about using material that emergent readers know or have heard. Often when we are introducing a new strategy, such as with this group, we pick materials that we hope kids will be a bit familiar with to build their confidence and comfort level in working with a new strategy.

"Nadjae, good predicting. Let's keep reading and see if you are correct. Okay, so we think the first word says *Jack*; let's look at the next word." Joan points to the space between words. "We know this will be the next word because there is always a space in between words. Look at this first letter, *a*. *A* often says /a/. The next letter is *n* and the last letter is *d*."

Caleb shouts out, "Hey, I know that word. It's one of our word wall words, see?" He jumps up, runs over to the word wall, grabs the sticky-note word, brings it back, and lays it down on the chart. "Yep, it's *and* all right!"

"So far we have *Jack and*; now let's look at the next word."

Nadjae jumps in. "It has to be *Jill*!"

"What would make you say that, Nadjae?"

"Look, the next word starts with a *J* that says /j/ just like *Jill*. So it must be *Jill*."

This is a great example of the approach this group has been taking to read text—looking at the first letter and at times the vowel but ignoring the rest of the letters in the word.

"Let's look at that. How could we be sure it says *Jill*?" The group is silent. After a time Joan says, "Remember the strategy we are working on is Use Beginning and Ending Sounds. Could we look at the ending sound and see if it matches *Jill*?"

The group bends over the chart, fingers pointing to the *l* at the end of the word.

"Let me show you again how this works." Again we say the first two sounds, /j/ and /i/; then pointing to the last letter in the word, *l*, we say the /l/ sound. "Let me blend that together and see if it says *Jill*. /Jill/ Oh my gosh, it does say *Jill*! I used the beginning sound and the ending sound to be sure that it said *Jill* instead of just guessing. So the title of this nursery rhyme is 'Jack and Jill.'"

"I knew it!" says Nadjae.

"Boys and girls, who remembers the accuracy strategy we worked on today?" Given the fact that we have been telling them throughout the lesson, it is always a surprise when children can't remember the strategy. But that is the case with this group, which is why we reinforce naming the strategies continuously. We never feel bad about repeating their goals and strategies over and over. After all, it is really their goal and strategy, so repeating ourselves to have them remember is worth every moment. We quickly read through the nursery rhyme together, with Joan pointing at the words and reading expressively. Everyone enjoys the rhythm and cadence of the classic nursery rhyme.

"So today, we started working with your new goal of accuracy, which means 'to read the words correctly.' The strategy we are working on right now to help you read words correctly is Use Beginning and Ending Sounds. I'm going to meet with you again tomorrow to reread this rhyme and work on our strategies." On the calendar in our Pensieve we write a shorthand note, which will remind us that one of the groups we are going to meet with is the group working on accuracy, Use Beginning and Ending Sounds.

"Now you are going to check in with your Daily Five choice that you would like to do for the rest of the round. Anytime you are reading to yourselves or with a partner today, I want you to try to practice looking at the beginning and ending sounds of the words in the stories you are reading and let me know tomorrow how it goes."

Goal: Comprehension

Strategy: Use Clues from Text Features (Third Graders)

Four boys, all transitional readers, each struggled with loving to read for a variety of reasons until they all found their way with nonfiction. They are enthralled by nature books, each delving with delight into the photos of weird and unexpected animals living in far regions of the world. The boys are able to decode and comprehend well; however, their lack of experience with nonfiction text features is inhibiting their ability to get the most out of the animal magazines, weird animal books, and other nonfiction texts they are reading.

Today, after the rest of the class has checked in with their Daily Five choice, we have an appointment to work with them as a small group. They join Joan on the green carpet, where she is armed with a tub of supplies in that area: copies of animal magazines for young people, clear acetate sheets, and water-soluble overhead pens.

"Hey, guys, I am so excited to work with you today! You all have the same goal, comprehension, and are all lovers of nonfiction and have been reading up a storm. I noticed that each of you has been reading from our tub of magazines and weird animal books, so for the next week or so, I am going to work with you all on your goal of comprehension and will teach you a new strategy: Use Text Features. Do any of you know what text features are?" No one has any idea what the term *text feature* means. "Text features are things in a book or magazine like titles, captions, headings, maps, and graphs. When we learn to pay attention to them as we read, we can better comprehend, or understand, what we are reading. I'm going to start today with some tools to model for you how readers use text features when they read to help them make sense of the text."

Joan takes out a magazine, opens it up to an interesting article, and then covers each side of the magazine with an acetate sheet.

"Often when we read nonfiction text like this, we love to look at the pictures, but we miss out on tons of information by not paying attention to some of the other text features on the page. I'm going to take this marker and circle some of the text features I am talking about."

Writing on the clear sheet, Joan first goes through and circles all the titles and headings on the page.

"Okay, check this out. The first thing you all typically do is look at the pictures. They are one text feature and can tell us a lot about the selection we are reading. By looking at the pictures, what do you think this article is going to be about?"

Eldar says, "It's going to be about bobcats and what they eat—I can tell from the pictures."

"So right after we look at the pictures, let's read the next text feature I have circled: titles and headings. You can tell where they are here, because their font, or type, is larger and darker. I'm going to read them aloud and think as I am reading about the pictures I just looked at."

Joan reads each title and heading she has circled, pausing to look at the pictures on the page.

Treven then says, "Hey, this isn't going to be about bobcats; it's about different kinds of lynx!"

"See how just looking at one of the text features, titles and headings, has already changed our comprehension of the selection? Okay, now I'm going to circle another text feature. This time it is the captions for the pictures. Do you notice that they are in dark print, smaller than the titles, and that most are under the pictures? However, check out this picture: it is right in the center of the magazine on the right page, but the caption isn't under it. Instead it is beside it on the left page. We can tell it is a caption because of the print, but we really had to look for it because it wasn't right below the photo. I am going to read the captions out loud, and we'll see what other information we can learn."

Joan reads the captions and learns that there are many types of lynx, in regions all over the world. One of the pictures is actually a world map. This map highlights the regions of the world where the lynx can be found. The map's caption indicates that each highlighted area is a region where lynx live. The boys are talking among themselves as if Joan is not there. Jared remarks that he had no idea why the map was there when he first looked at the page, but that now he "gets it."

"So we have looked at three text features so far: the pictures and maps, the titles and headings, and the captions. We have better comprehension or understanding of the selection already. First, we thought it was about bobcats, and then we learned it is actually about lynx and where they live.

"As I am looking at the text of this selection, I notice something that I think may be another text feature that could help me comprehend this piece better." Joan looks through the text and circles the dark words that are emphasized there.

"See all these dark words I circled? I am sure the author would not have made them dark unless they were important. Let's read each one and see if they give us more information that can help us comprehend the article."

Joan goes through and reads each one. The boys decide they need to read the whole article rather than the highlighted words alone.

"I understand you're feeling like you are ready to read the whole article. However, as a reader if there are words in the article that are highlighted, I always read them first so it gets my brain ready for the rest of the text.

"So here is what we are going to do. I've got the same supplies here for you that we just used, clear sheets and pens. I want you to work with someone else in this group, choose a page from a book or magazine that you both are interested in, and then go through and circle the text features. The whole time you do this I want you to talk together, just like we did, about how your thinking is changing and how you understand the article. I'm going to meet back with you in two days."

Joan writes that on the Pensieve calendar. "Bring your sheets and text and we'll talk about it together and then practice some more. You have some time right now to select your story and get started."

Goal: Expand Vocabulary

Strategy: Use Word Parts to Determine the Meaning of Words (Fifth Grade)

This is the first rotation of the day, and Gail is ready to meet with her first strategy group. She announces before beginning check-in for Daily Five, "I am going to meet with Josh, Sevilya, Anna, and Samuel. Please bring your reader's notebook and the book you are reading up to the floor. The rest of the class, let's have you check in with your choice for this round of Daily Five."

Students check in and go off to their independent work, and the strategy group joins Gail on the floor. These fifth-grade students are reading on grade level or above. As Gail looked at their assessments, she realized they comprehend details and can figure out cause and effect. But when they come to words they have never seen before, they lack strategies for understanding them.

"Hi, guys. This is our first day meeting together. You are all working on the goal of expanding vocabulary with the strategy Use Word Parts to Determine the Meaning of Words. We are going to be studying words and how they are put together, and watching for similar word patterns. When you come to words you don't know in your reading, you will be able to use this strategy to figure out their meaning."

"Turn to your goal section of your reading notebook and write down 'goal: expand vocabulary' and 'strategy: Use Word Parts to Determine the Meaning of Words.' Underneath that write this question: 'Do I know any of the word parts?' While you are writing, think about what this question means to our goal of expanding vocabulary."

Students write the question in their notebooks, and heads pop up as they finish.

Josh, the first one finished, says, "I already know this. Each word has small words or chunks in it to make up a new word, but my question is, like in the word *information*—I see the *in*, and the *tion*, but how would that help me with knowing the word?"

Gail thanks Josh for his response and then asks Sevilya what she thinks about the question "Do I know any of the word parts?"

"When I look at words, I already use those word parts to help me sound out the words, but I don't see how those word parts will help me understand the word."

The group nods in agreement.

"That is exactly what we are going to work on. We will be learning how the parts of words can help us figure out the meaning of the word.

"I brought in today's newspaper. I am going to read you an article about the Seattle Mariners. This is from last night's game. Did you hear the Mariners won, in extra innings? You know I love the team, and of course many of you do, too. I am going to read it twice. The first time let's see how the team played, and the second time let's look at some word parts.

"I am going to lay the paper down here on the floor and we'll all huddle close while I read the article."

Gail reads the article aloud, stopping periodically as the group savors the details of the win.

"Now, remember our goal is vocabulary and the strategy is Use Word Parts to Determine the Meaning of Words. For the next week, we are going to review word parts. To start off, you will be looking for compound words. Think what compound words mean to you and then lean over to your partner and give them an example."

Each student shares an example. Samuel says, "How is this going to help? I already know about compound words, but there are so many other words that aren't compound that I can't figure out."

"You are so right, Samuel," Gail says. "We are going to start with compound words to get our brains tuned in to seeing the parts of words. And then we will tune in to other chunks, like *un* and *re*, or *ful* and *less*—what we call prefixes and suffixes—and learn what they do to the meaning of words.

"I am going to read the first paragraph. While I read, I will circle any compound words I see. Follow along as I do this."

Gail reads the first paragraph and circles the words *outfielder, baseball*, and *shortstop*.

"Let's look at the word *outfielder*. I know that is a compound word because it has two small words I already know that are put together, *out* and *fielder*. I now ask myself the question you wrote down earlier, 'Do I know any of the word parts?' I know a *fielder* is someone who plays on the field of a baseball diamond, and that there are infielders who play close to the bases and outfielders who play away from the bases. Because this story is about baseball and I know a lot about baseball, I know an outfielder is a person who plays in the outfield. They are either the right fielder, the center fielder, or the left fielder. I used all of my background knowledge about baseball and the words *out* and *field* to figure it out. That was an easy one for me.

"Now it's your turn. I am going to read the next paragraph and you follow along. If you hear me say a compound word, raise your hand. I will stop, and you lean in and circle it on this newspaper."

Gail and the students read the rest of the article together, and the students circle compound words.

"Great—I think we got most of them. We just started the process of looking for word parts. We are going to start with the parts that are bigger and make sense to us, which are compound words. We are going to keep track of the words to see if we can make more sense of them, like how many parts there are and what happens when other parts are added, such as prefixes and suffixes.

"Boys and girls, each year you will learn many new words because we talk about them in class, but most of your words are going to come from your own reading. The one strategy that you can carry around with you at

Heather works with a small group; they have the same strategy focus, but each child has his or her own book.

all times is to use the word parts and then infer their meaning based on reading around the word.

"So here is what you are going to do today. Because there are four of you in this group, I want you to work together. You are going to take this newspaper somewhere in the room, and each of you is going to write down, in your reading notebook, all the compound words you found in this article. Then I want you to read them aloud to each other and try to figure out what they mean. Put a star next to the ones you know the meaning of and leave the ones you don't know the meaning of blank.

"I am going to meet with your group tomorrow to see how this worked, and then we will continue our search for compound words in your own stories. Remember, we are using these word parts to help us understand the words and what the text means.

"Are there any questions? Great thinking today!"

As you can see from these examples, we use a variety of texts, and meetings are short and tailored to the needs of the group. For more ideas on how to teach the CAFE strategies in strategy groups, you can look through the CAFE Ready Reference Guides in the appendix.

Last Words: The Never-Ending Stories of CAFE—Ours and Yours

We both started teaching more than two decades ago. At that time, teachers were just beginning to write about their experiences in their classrooms. After the dry "voice of God" literacy-methods textbooks we endured in college, we could hardly believe the gift of writing by authors such as Donald Graves, Nancie Atwell, Lucy Calkins, and Debbie Miller. It felt like those teachers were sitting with us over a cup of tea, telling us the stories of their teaching with humor, grit, and eloquence. Our teaching heroes were now real people to us, willing to share their successes as well as their struggles in a style that let us know we were all in this together, part of an incredible community of teachers who were learners, too. We'd close these books with a sigh, sorry the conversation was over.

We never thought we'd join the ranks of teachers publishing books about their teaching, and we never thought we'd see the day when conversations could continue well beyond the moment we turned the last page in a professional book. As you read these words, much time has passed since we wrote them. We've probably tweaked a form or two included in these pages and had a few epiphanies about new strategies we need to add to the CAFE Menu. We've certainly slapped our hands across our foreheads about some boneheaded idea in Chapter 2 or 4 we wish we could take back.

That's why we're delighted in this digital age that the conversation with you about CAFE doesn't have to end here—it may be just beginning. We hope you'll visit us at our website www.thedailycafe.com to read and view our latest learning and revised thinking about CAFE. We know we'll be sharing some of our new ideas through podcasts and print resources at www.stenhouse.com, so we hope you pop in for a visit there, too.

Teachers everywhere are adapting and adopting CAFE in their classrooms, putting their own stamp on the menu and discussing it on Web forums throughout the country and world. As we write these words, there are literally thousands of teachers who have formed and joined these online communities to support one another. You can find an active one yourself by using Google to search for "The Sisters Daily Five Literacy" or "The Sisters CAFE Literacy." We've talked about and written the story of how CAFE came to life in our classrooms. Now, through the power of the Web, we can't wait to read and see the story of how it comes to life in yours.

Appendix

The forms in this appendix are also included on the CD-ROM that accompanies the book. Blank forms can be filled in using Adobe Acrobat and then printed.

Launching CAFE Day 1

Whole-Group Strategy Lesson One	Whole-Group Strategy Lesson Two	Whole-Group Strategy Lesson Three
Read a picture book. Model and teach the comprehension strategy Check for Understanding. Introduce and explain the purpose and meaning of the heading Comprehension on the CAFE Menu board. In front of the students, write the strategy Check for Understanding on a blank CAFE Menu card and post it on the CAFE Menu under Comprehension.	Read a picture book. Review and model Check for Understanding, point to this card on CAFE Menu board, and continue reading. Model and teach Cross Checking. Explain the purpose and meaning of the heading Accuracy. In front of the students, write the strategy Cross Checking on a blank CAFE Menu card and post it on the CAFE Menu under Accuracy.	Read a picture book or chapter book. Review and model Check for Understanding, point to the card on the CAFE Menu, continue reading. Review and model Cross Checking, point to card on CAFE Menu board, continue reading. Model and teach Tune In to Interesting Words. Explain the purpose of the heading Expand Vocabulary. In front of the students, write the strategy Tune In to Interesting Words on a blank CAFE Menu card and post it on the CAFE Menu board under Expand Vocabulary.

While we are launching Daily Five, we are also launching CAFE. These are the lessons we teach in a whole-group format to all of our students each time we read a picture book or chapter book. Eventually the CAFE lessons will be our Daily Five Strategy Lessons—CAFE is fully integrated into Daily Five. In other words, every time we end a round of Daily Five and prepare to begin a new one is an opportunity for a CAFE Strategy Lesson.

For the first few days of school, before we assess all of our students, we teach and reinforce reading strategies that are fundamental to the reading process. For many students, these strategies are a review of what they already know, which is not a bad teaching strategy for the first days of a new grade. It reminds us of going to a conference where the speaker says some things that we are already doing in our teaching. We feel affirmed and secure in our skills, and then are more open to listening to the new ideas presented.

Launching CAFE Day 2

Whole-Group Strategy Lesson One	Whole-Group Strategy Lesson Two	Whole-Group Strategy Lesson Three
Read a picture or chapter book. Choose one or two spots in the book to review the strategy of Check for Understanding and point to the card on the CAFE Menu board. Model and teach the Comprehension strategy of Back Up and Reread, a fix-up strategy when Check for Understanding doesn't work. In front of the students, write the strategy Back Up and Reread on a blank CAFE Menu card and post it on the CAFE Menu under Comprehension.	Read a picture or chapter book. Review and model Check for Understanding, point to the card on the CAFE Menu board, and continue reading. Review and model Cross Checking, and refer to this card on the CAFE Menu board. Review and model Tune In to Interesting Words, pointing to the card on the CAFE Menu board.	Read a picture or chapter book. Continue to stop at one or two spots in the book to review each of the strategies: Check for Understanding, Cross Checking, Tune In to Interesting Words, and Back Up and Reread.

Launching CAFE Days 3–6

Whole-Group Strategy Lesson One

Introduce and teach Read Appropriate-Level Texts That Are a Good Fit.

Explain the purpose and meaning of the CAFE heading Fluency.

In front of the students, write the strategy Read Appropriate-Level Texts That Are a Good Fit on a blank CAFE Menu card and post it on the CAFE Menu under Fluency.

During the next three to six days, continue to stop a few times while reading aloud to review each of the strategies: Check for Understanding, Cross Checking, Tune In to Interesting Words, Back Up and Reread, Read Appropriate-Level Texts That Are a Good Fit. Then review these strategies as needed.

Our goal is threefold:

1. Model and teach these five foundational strategies, knowing children must see and hear them often before they can begin to use them.
2. Anchor these strategies to the CAFE Menu board in our classroom. Teaching children to view the menu as a visual aid to be used while reading helps them to remember strategies.
3. Model for students that readers use many strategies at one time while reading.

Whole-Group Strategy Lesson Two

Continue reviewing all strategies introduced to this point.

One-on-One Assessing

As students are building stamina with Daily Five, we stay out of their way until they exhibit about seven to fifteen minutes of stamina. At this time, we start our individual assessments to find out exactly what skills and strategies each individual student needs and also their area of strength. We begin to build our flexible groups by using the Strategy Groups form (see pages 21, 22, and 147 for a description).

Whole-Group Strategy Lesson Three

Continue reviewing all strategies introduced to this point.

One-on-One Assessing

While students are practicing their stamina during Daily Five, we assess one student at a time using the following steps we call From Assessment to Instruction (see page 39):

1. Assess individual student.
2. Discuss with student what he or she knows about him- or herself as a reader as well as what you know and have learned about him or her as a reader, using CAFE Menu as a reference (see pages 24 and 143).
3. Set goal and identify reading strategies with student.
4. Student declares goal on CAFE Menu.
5. Teacher fills out Strategy Groups form (see pages 21, 22, and 147).
6. Teacher fills out individual Reading Conference sheet (see pages 25, 148, and 149).
7. Instruction.

Launching CAFE Days 7–11

Whole-Group Strategy Lesson One

Model and teach the comprehension strategy of Monitor and Fix Up.

From now on, we ask students to write on the strategy cards. We write the strategy Monitor and Fix Up on a sticky note and hand it to one of the students along with a blank CAFE Menu card. We ask the student to copy the strategy on the card, add a visual to help us remember the strategy, and finally, write his or her name. Then, in front of the class, the student posts Monitor and Fix Up on the CAFE Menu under Comprehension.

Review this strategy for the next few days and then as needed.

If required to use a basal, teach a comprehension strategy from the basal, write the strategy on a blank CAFE strategy card, and post the strategy on the CAFE Menu under Comprehension.

One-on-One Assessing

Use Assessment to Instruction steps to assess one or two students (see page 39).

Our goal is to assess one or two students each day. By the end of the first month of school, we typically have assessed all of our students and all components of Daily Five are up and going.

Whole-Group Strategy Lesson Two

Model and teach Voracious Reading as it relates to Fluency.

Write the strategy Voracious Reading on a sticky note and hand it to one of the students along with a blank CAFE Menu card. The student copies the strategy on the card, adds a visual to help us remember the strategy, and finally, writes his or her name. Then, in front of the class, the student posts Voracious Reading on the CAFE Menu under Fluency.

Review this strategy for the next few days and then as needed.

If required to use a basal, teach an accuracy, fluency, or vocabulary strategy from the basal. Write the strategy on a blank CAFE strategy card and post the strategy on the CAFE Menu under the correct heading.

One-on-One Assessing

Use Assessment to Instruction steps to assess one or two students (see page 39).

Our goal is to assess one or two students each day. By the end of the first month of school, we typically have assessed all of our students and all components of Daily Five are up and going.

Whole-Group Strategy Lesson Three

Model and teach Voracious Reading as it relates to Vocabulary.

Explain the purpose and meaning of the CAFE heading of Expand Vocabulary.

Write the strategy Voracious Reading on a sticky note and hand it to one of the students along with a blank CAFE Menu card. The student copies the strategy on the card, adds a visual to help us remember the strategy, and finally, writes his or her name. Then, in front of the class, the student posts Voracious Reading on the CAFE Menu under Expand Vocabulary.

Review this strategy for the next few days and then as needed.

If required to use a basal, teach an accuracy, fluency, or vocabulary strategy from the basal. Write the strategy on a blank CAFE strategy card, and post the strategy on the CAFE Menu under the correct heading.

One-on-One Assessing

Use Assessment to Instruction steps to assess one or two students (see page 39).

Our goal is to assess one or two students each day. By the end of the first month of school, we typically have assessed all of our students and all components of Daily Five are up and going.

Launching CAFE Days 12–16

Whole-Group Strategy Lesson One

Model and teach the comprehension strategy of Use Prior Knowledge to Connect with Text.

Write the strategy Use Prior Knowledge to Connect with Text on a sticky note and hand it to one of the students along with a blank CAFE Menu card. The student copies the strategy on a blank CAFE Menu card, adds a visual to help us remember the strategy, and finally, writes his or her name. Then, in front of the class, the student posts Use Prior Knowledge to Connect with Text on the CAFE Menu under Comprehension.

Review this strategy for the next few days and then review as needed.

If required to use a basal, teach a comprehension strategy from the basal, write the strategy on a blank CAFE strategy card, and post the strategy on the CAFE Menu under Comprehension.

One-on-One Assessing

Use Assessment to Instruction steps to assess one or two students (see page 39).

Our goal is to assess one or two students each day. By the end of the first month of school, we typically have assessed all of our students and all components of Daily Five are up and going.

Whole-Group Strategy Lesson Two

Review, continue to teach, and reinforce the strategy Read Appropriate-Level Texts That Are a Good Fit. Point to this card on the CAFE Menu board.

If required to use a basal, teach an accuracy, fluency, or vocabulary strategy from the basal. Write the strategy on a blank CAFE strategy card, and post the strategy on the CAFE Menu under the correct heading.

One-on-One Assessing

Use Assessment to Instruction steps to assess one or two students (see page 39).

Our goal is to assess one or two students each day. By the end of the first month of school, we typically have assessed all of our students and all components of Daily Five are up and going.

Whole-Group Strategy Lesson Three

Review, continue to teach, and reinforce the strategies posted on the CAFE Menu board. Point to this card on the CAFE Menu board as you refer to them.

If required to use a basal, teach an accuracy, fluency, or vocabulary strategy from the basal. Write the strategy on a blank CAFE strategy card, and post the strategy on the CAFE Menu under the correct heading.

One-on-One Assessing

Use Assessment to Instruction steps to assess one or two students (see page 39).

Our goal is to assess one or two students each day. By the end of the first month of school, we typically have assessed all of our students and all components of Daily Five are up and going.

Launching CAFE Days 17–21

Whole-Group Strategy Lesson One

Model and teach the comprehension strategy of Make a Picture or Mental Image.

Write the strategy Make a Picture or Mental Image on a sticky note and hand it to one of the students along with a blank CAFE Menu card. The student copies the strategy on a blank CAFE menu card, adds a visual to help us remember the strategy, and finally, writes his or her name. Then, in front of the class, the student posts Make a Picture or Mental Image on the CAFE Menu under Comprehension.

Review this strategy for the next few days, and then review as needed.

If required to use a basal, teach a comprehension strategy from the basal, write the strategy on a blank CAFE strategy card, and post the strategy on the CAFE Menu under Comprehension.

One-on-One Assessing

Uses Assessment to Instruction steps to assess one or two students (see page 39).

Our goal is to assess one or two students each day. By the end of the first month of school, we typically have assessed all of our students and all components of Daily Five are up and going.

Whole-Group Strategy Lesson Two

Review, continue to teach, and reinforce the strategy Read Appropriate-Level Texts That Are a Good Fit. Point to this card on the CAFE Menu board.

If required to use a basal, teach an accuracy, fluency, or vocabulary strategy from the basal. Write the strategy on a blank CAFE strategy card and post the strategy on the CAFE Menu under the correct heading.

One-on-One Assessing

Uses Assessment to Instruction steps to assess one or two students (see page 39).

Our goal is to assess one or two students each day. By the end of the first month of school, we typically have assessed all of our students and all components of Daily Five are up and going.

Whole-Group Strategy Lesson Three

Review, continue to teach, and reinforce the strategies posted on the CAFE Menu board. Point to these cards on the CAFE Menu board as you refer to them.

If required to use a basal, teach an accuracy, fluency, or vocabulary strategy from the basal. Write the strategy on a blank CAFE strategy card, and post the strategy on the CAFE Menu under the correct heading.

One-on-One Assessing

Uses Assessment to Instruction steps to assess one or two students (see page 39).

Our goal is to assess one or two students each day. By the end of the first month of school, we typically have assessed all of our students and all components of Daily Five are up and going.

Launching CAFE Days 22–26

Whole-Group Strategy Lesson One

Based on our students' assessments, we take the skills and strategies all of our students need and map them out on what we call a curriculum calendar (see page 146). These strategies become what we teach during our whole-group lessons. We also use this map to write down a plan for teaching our state standards.

Critical to this planning and mapping of skills is thinking. We filter each planned lesson with this question: Do all of my students still need this skill or strategy? If they do, we teach it in a whole-group format; if not, we will teach it to a small group of students who need the strategy or just teach it to the individuals who need it.

If required to use a basal, teach a comprehension strategy from the basal, write the strategy on a blank CAFE strategy card, and post the strategy on the CAFE Menu under Comprehension.

Flexible Group

Once we have assessed all of our students and know each student's strengths and areas of need, we begin meeting with students in small flexible groups based

(continued on next page)

Whole-Group Strategy Lesson Two

Based on our students' assessments, we take the skills and strategies all of our students need and map them out on what we call a curriculum calendar (see page 146). These strategies become what we teach during our whole-group lessons. We also use this map to write down a plan for teaching our state standards.

Critical to this planning and mapping of skills is thinking. We filter each planned lesson with this question: Do all of my students still need this skill or strategy? If they do, we teach it in a whole-group format; if not, we will teach it to a small group of students who need the strategy or just teach it to the individuals who need it.

If required to use a basal, teach an accuracy, fluency, or vocabulary strategy from the basal. Write the strategy on a blank CAFE strategy card, and post the strategy on the CAFE Menu under the correct heading.

Intermediate Students

If you are teaching intermediate students, you may be ready to go from three rounds of Daily Five down to two. When that happens, we typically teach

(continued on next page)

Whole-Group Strategy Lesson Three

Based on our students' assessments, we take the skills and strategies all of our students need and map them out on what we call a curriculum calendar (see page 146). These strategies become what we teach during our whole-group lessons. We also use this map to write down a plan for teaching our state standards.

Critical to this planning and mapping of skills is thinking. We filter each planned lesson with this question: Do all of my students still need this skill or strategy? If they do, we teach it in a whole-group format; if not, we will teach it to a small group of students who need the strategy or just teach it to the individuals who need it.

If required to use a basal, teach an accuracy, fluency, or vocabulary strategy from the basal. Write the strategy on a blank CAFE strategy card and post the strategy on the CAFE Menu under the correct heading.

Flexible Group

Once we have assessed all of our students and know each student's strengths and areas of need, we begin meeting with students in small flexible groups based

(continued on next page)

Launching CAFE Days 22–26 *(continued)*

<table>
<tr>
<td>on like need. We refer to our Strategy Groups form (see pages 21, 22, and 147 for a description) that we filled out while assessing our students.
We typically meet with one group during each Daily Five rotation.

Individual Conferences
Using the information gathered from assessing each student, also meet with three or four students during each round of Daily Five.</td>
<td>a comprehension lesson during our first strategy lesson and a writing lesson during our second strategy lesson. Since students now have about thirty to forty minutes of stamina, each round of Daily Five is longer.
When thinking of the CAFE Menu skills and strategies, if children at this level need accuracy or fluency, they are taught individually or in a flexible group. Vocabulary is typically taught during our read-aloud.

Flexible Group
Once we have assessed all of our students and know each student's strengths and areas of need, we begin meeting with students in small flexible groups based on like need. We refer to our Strategy Groups form (see pages 21, 22, and 147 for a description) that we filled out while assessing our students.
We typically meet with one group during each Daily Five rotation.

Individual Conferences
Using the information gathered from assessing each student, meet with three or four students during each round of Daily Five.</td>
<td>on like need. We refer to our Strategy Groups form (see pages 21, 22, and 147 for a description) that we filled out while assessing our students.
We typically meet with one group during each Daily Five rotation.

Individual Conferences
Using the information gathered from assessing each student, also meet with three or four students during each round of Daily Five.</td>
</tr>
</table>

Typical Literacy Block Schedule of First Week

Primary and Intermediate

8:50–9:00	Day begins, gather on rug, take attendance, opening poem
Literacy Block	
9:00–9:10	Whole-group strategy lesson, three ways to read a book
9:10–9:40	Launching Daily Five
9:40–9:45	Brain and body break—songs, poems, chants
9:45–10:00	CAFE Strategy Lesson One with a picture book
10:00–10:15	Brain and body break—songs, poems, chants
10:15–10:30	CAFE Strategy Lesson Two with a picture book
10:30–10:35	Brain and body break—songs, poems, chants
10:35–10:50	CAFE Strategy Lesson Three with a picture book
10:50–10:55	Brain and body break—songs, poems, chants
10:55–11:25	Shared writing/writer's workshop introduction
11:25–11:30	Ready for lunch
11:30–12:10	Lunch and recess

Times are approximate.

Typical Literacy Block Schedule of First Week

Primary

8:50–9:00	Day begins, gather on rug, take attendance, opening poem
Literacy Block	
9:00–9:10	Whole-group strategy lesson, three ways to read a book
9:10–9:40	Launching Daily Five
9:40–9:45	Brain and body break—songs, poems, chants
9:45–10:00	CAFE Strategy Lesson One with a picture book
10:00–10:15	Brain and body break—songs, poems, chants
10:15–10:30	CAFE Strategy Lesson Two with a picture book
10:30–10:35	Brain and body break—songs, poems, chants
10:35–10:50	CAFE Strategy Lesson Three with a picture book
10:50–10:55	Brain and body break—songs, poems, chants
10:55–11:25	Shared writing/writer's workshop introduction
11:25–11:30	Ready for lunch
11:30–12:10	Lunch and recess

Times are approximate.

Typical Literacy Block Schedule Weeks 2–6

Primary

8:50–9:00	Day begins, gather on rug, take attendance, opening poem
Literacy Block	
9:00–9:15	CAFE Strategy Lesson—Comprehension with a picture book
9:15–9:25	Round One of Daily Five—Teacher conducts individual assessments
9:25–9:30	Brain and body break
9:30–9:40	CAFE Strategy Lesson—Accuracy
9:40–9:50	Round Two of Daily Five—Teacher conducts individual assessments
9:50–9:55	Brain and body break
9:55–10:05	CAFE Strategy Lesson—Fluency/Expand Vocabulary
10:05–10:15	Round Three of Daily Five—Teacher conducts individual assessments
10:15–10:20	Brain and body break
10:20–10:30	Round Four of Daily Five—Teacher conducts individual assessments
10:30–10:35	Brain and body break
10:35–10:40	Preteaching of Daily Five skills
10:40–10:50	Round Five of Daily Five—Teacher conducts individual assessments
10:50–10:55	Share/review of strategies
10:55–11:25	Shared writing/writer's workshop
11:25–11:30	Ready for lunch
11:30–12:10	Lunch and recess

Times are approximate and vary as children build stamina.

Typical Literacy Block Schedule Weeks 6+

or After Daily Five or Literacy Routines Are in Place
Primary

8:50–9:00	Day begins, gather on rug, take attendance, opening poem

Literacy Block

9:00–9:15	CAFE Strategy Lesson—Comprehension with a picture book
9:15–9:35	Round One of Daily Five—Teacher works with small group, then confers with three to four students
9:35–9:45	CAFE Strategy Lesson—Accuracy
9:45–10:05	Round Two of Daily Five—Teacher works with small group, then confers with three to four students
10:05–10:15	CAFE Strategy Lesson—Fluency/Expand Vocabulary
10:15–10:35	Round Three of Daily Five—Teacher works with small group, then confers with three to four students
10:35–10:45	Share/review of strategies
10:45–11:25	Shared writing/writer's workshop
11:25–11:30	Ready for lunch
11:30–12:10	Lunch and recess

Times are approximate and vary.

Typical Literacy Block Schedule Weeks 6+

or After Daily Five or Literacy Routines Are in Place
Intermediate

8:50–9:00	Day begins, gather on rug, take attendance, opening poem

Literacy Block

9:00–9:25	CAFE Strategy Lesson—Comprehension with a picture book
9:25–10:10	Round One of Daily Five—Teacher works with small group, then confers with five to eight students
10:10–10:35	Strategy Lesson—Writing
10:35–11:15	Round Two of Daily Five—Teacher works with small group, then confers with five to eight students
11:15–11:30	Share/review strategies
11:30–12:10	Lunch and recess

Times are approximate and vary.

The Literacy CAFE Menu

Comprehension I understand what I read	**Accuracy** I can read the words	**Fluency** I can read accurately, with expression, and understand what I read	**Expand Vocabulary** I know, find, and use interesting words
Strategies Check for understanding Back up and reread Monitor and fix up Retell the story Use prior knowledge to connect with text Make a picture or mental image Ask questions throughout the reading process Predict what will happen; use text to confirm Infer and support with evidence Use text features (titles, headings, captions, graphic features) Summarize text; include sequence of main events Use main idea and supporting details to determine importance Determine and analyze author's purpose and support with text Recognize literacy elements (genre, plot, character, setting, problem/resolution, theme) Recognize and explain cause-and-effect relationships Compare and contrast within and between text	***Strategies*** Cross checking . . . Do the pictures and/or words look right? Do they sound right? Do they make sense? Use the pictures . . . Do the words and pictures match? Use beginning and ending sounds Blend sounds; stretch and reread Flip the sound Chunk letters and sounds together Skip the word, then come back Trade a word/guess a word that makes sense	***Strategies*** Voracious reading Read appropriate-level texts that are a good fit Reread text Practice common sight words and high-frequency words Adjust and apply different reading rates to match text Use punctuation to enhance phrasing and prosody (end marks, commas, etc.)	***Strategies*** Voracious reading Tune in to interesting words and use new vocabulary in speaking and writing Use pictures, illustrations, and diagrams Use word parts to determine the meaning of words (prefixes, suffixes, origins, abbreviations, etc.) Use prior knowledge and context to predict and confirm meaning Ask someone to define the word for you Use dictionaries, thesauruses, and glossaries as tools

Behaviors That Support Reading

Get started right away Stay in one place Work quietly Read the whole time Increase stamina Select and read good-fit books

Keeping Track: Reading Writing

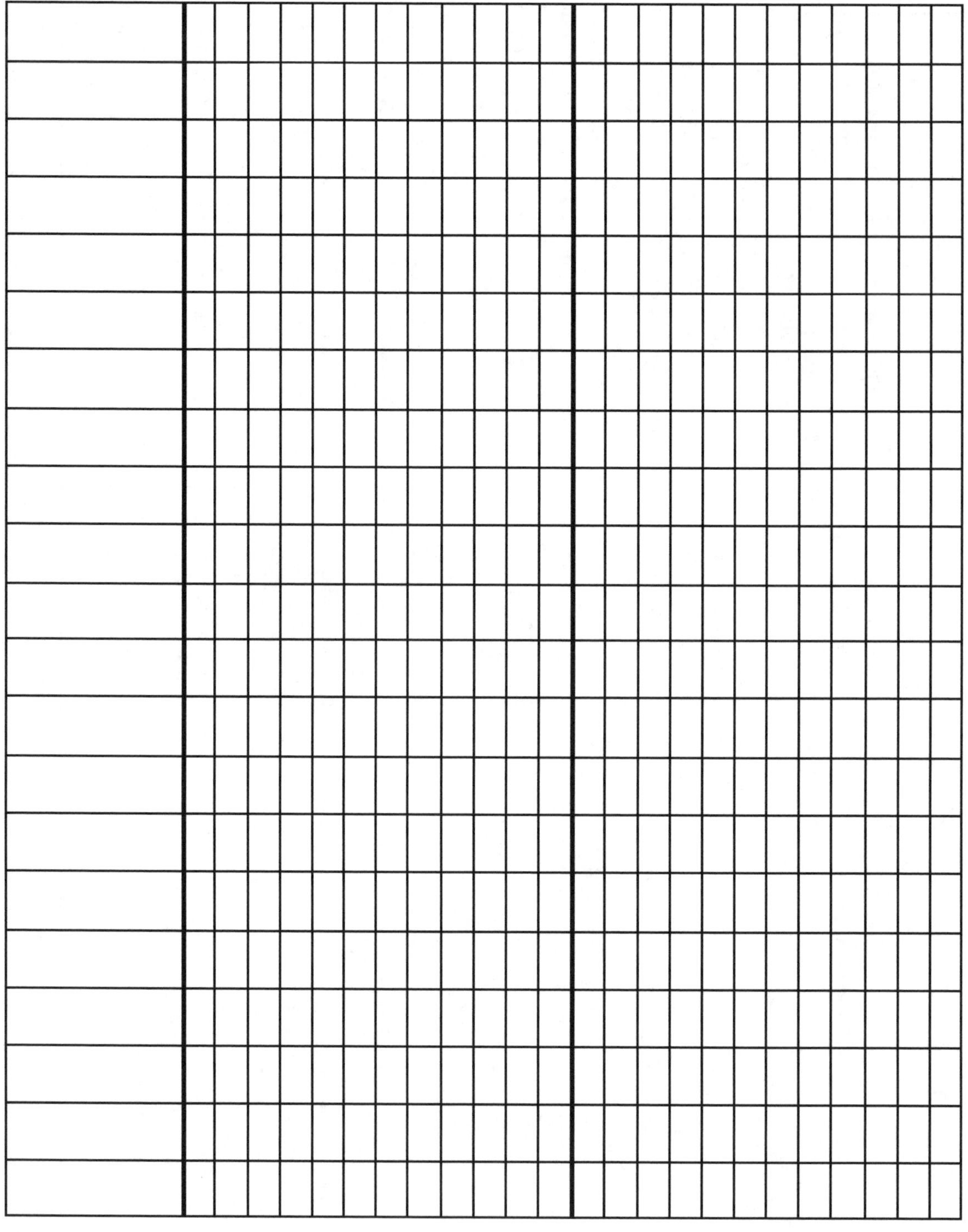

Calendar

The image below shows the main screen of the Google Calendar website, where you can create your own customized calendars for free. To use the website, go to: http://www.google.com/googlecalendar/overview.html.

Welcome to Google Calendar

Calendar Home
Overview
What's New
Take the Tour
Event Publisher Guide
Privacy Information
For Work or School
Help Center

Want to try it out?
Sign in now

Simplify. Organize. (And relax.) Organizing your schedule shouldn't be a burden. That's why we've created Google Calendar – our free online shareable calendar service. With Google Calendar, it's easy to keep track of all your life's important events – birthdays, reunions, little league games, doctor's appointments – all in one place.

Using Google Calendar, you can add events and invitations effortlessly, share with friends and family (or keep things to yourself), and search across the web for events you might enjoy. It's organizing made easy.

Gmail Integration
Gmail now recognizes when messages mention events, and you can add those events to your calendar with just a couple clicks.

Quick Add
Just click a spot on your calendar (or use the Quick Add link) and start typing to add a new event

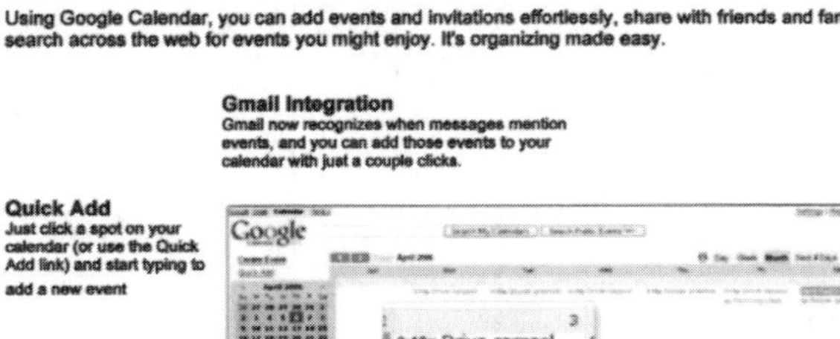

Calendar Sharing
View calendars that others have shared with you, and let your friends and family see your agenda.

Invitations
Send invitations for any event on your calendar by adding guests

Reminders
Never forget another event again. You can even get reminders sent right to your mobile phone.

Take the Google Calendar Tour

Features

Calendar Sharing: Set up a calendar for your company softball team, and share it with the whole roster. (Your shortstop will never forget about practice again.) Or share with friends and family so you can view each other's schedules side by side.

Invitations: Create event invitations, send them to friends, and keep track of people's responses and comments, all in one place. Your friends can receive your invitation and post responses even if they don't use Google Calendar themselves.

Quick Add: Click anywhere on your calendar where an event belongs (or use the Quick Add link), and start typing. Google Calendar understands whole phrases like "Brunch with mom at Java Cafe 11am on Saturday," and will pop new events right into your agenda.

Gmail Integration: Add your friend's Super Bowl party to your calendar without ever leaving your Gmail inbox. Gmail now recognizes events mentioned in emails.

Search: Find the date of the Baxter family BBQ (you knew it was sometime this summer). Or, search public calendars to discover new events you're interested in and add them to your own calendar.

Mobile Access: Receive event reminders and notifications on your mobile phone.

Event Publishing: Share your organization's events with the world. Learn more with our Event Publisher Guide.

Curriculum Calendar

Month	Week 1	Week 2	Week 3	Week 4
Comprehension Strategy				
Accuracy Strategy				
Phonics/Spelling Skill				
Fluency Strategy				
Vocabulary				
Anchor Books				
Writing Skill/Strategy				
Writing Form				
Math Strategy				
Social Studies				
Science				
Health				
Technology				
Assessment				

Strategy Groups and Instruction

Goal	Strategy	Names	Touch Points
Date	Lesson		
Goal	Strategy	Names	Touch Points
Date	Lesson		
Goal	Strategy	Names	Touch Points
Date	Lesson		

Reading Conference

Goals	Student Strengths
• •	• •

Date Touch Point	Observation and Instruction	Next Steps to Meet Goal
Date Touch Point		
Date Touch Point		
Date Touch Point		
Date Touch Point		
Date Touch Point		
Date Touch Point		

Reading Conference with Icons

Goals • •		**Student Strengths** • •
Date Touch Point	**Observation and Instruction**	**Next Steps to Meet Goal**
Touch Point		Next
Touch Point		Next
Touch Point		Next
Touch Point		Next
Touch Point		Next
Touch Point		Next

Writing Conference

Goals	**Student Strengths**
•	•
•	•

Date	**Observation and Instruction**	**Next Steps to Meet Goal**

Coaching Toward a Target

Productive, Effective, Focused Teaching and Learning

1. Check calendar for appointments.
2. Prepare (30 seconds)
   Review your conferring notes for the student's strengths and strategy focus.
3. Observe (1 minute) *"[Student], please read so I can listen in; then tell me about yourself as a reader."*
   Observe the student. Is he or she applying the skill/strategy taught or reinforced last time you met?
   What is the student doing well with his or her strategy/skill application?
   Record this on the conferring sheet.
4. Reinforce and Teach (1 minute)
   "I noticed ________ ; what did you notice? Today we are going to ________."
   Verbally share with student your observations of what he or she was doing well.
   Teach or reinforce the skill or strategy you feel is just right for the student now by
   - explicit explanation,
   - modeling,
   - thinking aloud,
   - offering advice.
5. Practice (1 minute) *"Now it is your turn. You try . . . "*
   Ask the student to practice the skill/strategy while you listen in.
6. Plan (30 seconds) *"This is what I am hearing, and because of that, this may be our next step."*
   Based on today's teaching and learning, decide and agree together what the next step will be. It isn't uncommon for students to need continued practice with the previous strategy.
   Write this plan on the coaching sheet.
7. Encourage (15 seconds)
   Just before you leave the student, encourage him or her to continue to practice the skill taught or reinforced today.
   Student should articulate the goal.

- The times above serve as guidelines, and though it isn't necessary to strictly adhere to them, they will give you a general idea so you can keep your conferences focused and brief.
- Each step above may be shorter or longer, depending on what the child is doing that day, and where you are in the gradual release of teaching the skills or strategies to the student.
- Remember that brief, focused conferences that occur frequently are considerably more beneficial than sporadic, lengthy ones.

Word Collector

Aa	Bb	Cc	Dd	Ee
Ff	Gg	Hh	Ii	Jj
Kk	Ll	Mm	Nn	Oo
Pp	Qq	Rr	Ss	Tt
Uu	Vv	Ww	Xx, Yy	Zz

From Assessment to Conferring: Sample Needs and Strategies

What We Are Seeing	Potential Goals	Possible Strategy	Alternative Strategy
Reading too quickly	Fluency	Adjust and apply different reading rates to match text	Phrasing, use punctuation
Leaving off ends of words	Accuracy	Cross checking	Chunk letters together
Little expression, lacks prosody, and omits punctuation	Fluency	Phrasing, using punctuation	Voracious reading
Can't remember what was read	Comprehension	Check for understanding	Retell or summarize Make a picture or mental image Determine importance using theme, main ideas, and supporting details
Stalls on words	Accuracy	Skip the word, then come back	Blend sounds; stretch and reread
Student jumps right into reading story, then lacks understanding	Comprehension	Use prior knowledge to connect with text	Ask questions while reading Make connections to text
Doesn't remember details but understands the main idea	Comprehension	Retell the story	Recognize literary elements
Doesn't stick with a book	Reading Behaviors Book Selection	Read appropriate-level text Choose good-fit books	Voracious reading
Chooses books that are too hard	Reading Behaviors Fluency Expand Vocabulary Comprehension Accuracy	Read appropriate-level text	Ask, Does this make sense?
Can comprehend literally but can't read between the lines	Comprehension	Infer and support with evidence	Ask questions while reading Predict what will happen; use text to confirm
Reads words with correct letters but wrong sounds	Accuracy	Flip the sound	Cross checking
Sounds out each individual letter	Accuracy	Chunk letters together	Blend sounds
Beginning reader, knows few words but most letter sounds	Fluency Accuracy	Practice common sight words and high-frequency words	Blend sounds; stretch and reread
Doesn't remember details from nonfiction	Comprehension	Use text features (titles, headings, captions, graphic features)	Determine and analyze author's purpose and support with text
Doesn't understand the text because does not understand key word in selection	Expand Vocabulary	Tune in to interesting words	Reread to clarify the meaning of a word Ask someone to define the word for you

Ready Reference Form

Goal: Comprehension	Strategy: Check for Understanding
Definition	A comprehension strategy that teaches children to stop frequently and check, or monitor, whether they understand what they are reading. This typically is a quick summary of what they've read, starting with "who" and "what."
Why Children Need This Strategy	Often as beginning readers, children are so aware of reading accurately that they forget to take time and think about what they are reading, checking to see whether they understand the text. Advanced readers can develop the habit of reading through text without monitoring whether they were unaware of the Check for Understanding strategy as beginning readers.
Secret to Success	Knowing when we read that we must think about the story and realize what the author is trying to tell us or what we are learning from the book. Readers stop frequently to check for understanding or to ask who and what.
How We Teach It	This vital strategy is not only one of the first we introduce, but also one we model each and every day of the school year. ◆ Modeling during our read-aloud we stop periodically and say, "Let me see if I remember what I just read. I am going to start by thinking of who the story was about and what happened." ◆ We continue to stop periodically and talk through the "who" and "what," usually about three or four times during each read-aloud. ◆ After two or three times of modeling this for students, we start asking them to answer the "who" and the "what" through "listen and talk," asking one student to do it for the whole class and then expecting children to do it on their own. Language we use: "Stop often to check for understanding before you read any further." "**Who** did you just read about and **what** just happened?" "How often did you stop to check for understanding? After each sentence, after each paragraph, at the end of each page?" "Was your brain talking to you while you read?" "Are you finding you are understanding what you are reading?" "What do you do if you don't remember?"
Troubleshooting	We had a parent cut out large check marks, approximately 7 inches long, from balsa wood. Often we provide these check marks to students as a reminder to stop and check for understanding. They work particularly well when partners are reading together and working on Check for Understanding. The person listening to his or her partner read has the job of holding the check mark. When the reader comes to the end of a page or paragraph, the check-mark holder checks for understanding what the reader just read. On one side of the check marks we write, "Check for Understanding" and on the other side, "Who and what." For examples of a whole-group and individual conference using this strategy, see pages 30, 70, and 72.

Ready Reference Form

Goal: Comprehension	**Strategy: Back Up and Reread**
Definition	When meaning breaks down, going back and rereading again to understand the meaning of the selection.
Why Children Need This Strategy	Back Up and Reread is one of those consistent strategies good readers use because it works. Once readers back up and read the passage again, they usually read it more slowly, with more intention and focus, thus allowing their brain to absorb the meaning of what is read or the lack of meaning.
Secret to Success	Readers must be aware when text is not making sense, or when they are just reading the words but not thinking about what they are reading. When they are using this strategy, they may have to slow down. They always have to think about what they are reading. Pay attention to what is read, sometimes slowing down to read it more slowly so as to think about the meaning.
How We Teach It	We are always surprised to realize how often we back up and reread as adult readers. Our favorite way to teach this strategy, like so many others, is through modeling. Each and every time we pick up a book to read to children, inevitably we reread for a variety of reasons. At first we point out to the class each time we reread and what we were thinking when we did it. Soon they are pointing it out for us! Often we have a student in the class who will be the "Back Up and Reread counter." Each time we elicit the strategy, they quietly put up a finger. At the end of the story, they report the number of times we reread. "Did that make sense? What does a reader do when the text doesn't make sense? Even when you use other strategies like Cross Checking, you also need to back up and reread." "When you back up and reread, try rereading a bit more slowly. Often it can help you understand what you are reading if you slow it down."
Troubleshooting	Some children don't want to take the time to back up and reread. They want to read quickly and move on. The more we model backing up to reread, the more children will use the strategy as well. For an example of this strategy, see page 38.

Ready Reference Form

Goal: Comprehension	Strategy: Monitor and Fix Up
Definition	Readers stop and think if what they are reading makes sense, whether they understand what is happening in the story, or what the selection is about. If meaning breaks down, the reader has strategies to go back and fix it.
Why Children Need This Strategy	Readers who monitor their own reading know and use specific strategies when meaning breaks down, and fix their reading to enhance their comprehension.
Secret to Success	Readers must think while they are reading, constantly asking themselves, "Does this make sense?" If they don't know what is happening, they fix up their reading by using specific strategies.
How We Teach It	We model for students the language we use to monitor our meaning. It may sound like this: "Part of what I just read doesn't make sense. I am going to stop and ask myself some questions to see if I can figure it out. For example, 'Who is this story about? What is happening in this story? What is the author trying to tell me?' Asking these questions causes me to stop and think about what I am reading. "If after I have monitored or thought about what I was reading I am still lost or can't figure it out, I either reread the selection and try a fix-up strategy or I read on and try stopping again later in the passage. If it still doesn't make sense after the second attempt, I will have to ask someone for clarification or choose a book that is more appropriate to my level." Some fix-up strategies readers use: Summarize text. Go back and adjust the rate at which we read. Reread the text while thinking carefully. Read on to see whether the information becomes clear. Skim and scan the selection to gain meaning. Ask for help.
Troubleshooting	One way to help students with this strategy is to ask them to create a list of their favorite fix-up strategies they use when meaning breaks down. Once this list is made, it is easy to call students' attention to these strategies during individual conferences to remind them that they have the knowledge to fix up their reading. Through the conference we can check in and coach them to use the strategies until they become a habit.

Ready Reference Form

Goal: Comprehension	**Strategy: Retell the Story**
Definition	An accounting of a story's key points, told in sequence. A retelling usually includes characters, setting, problems, and solution or the main ideas of the text. It involves telling what is important in the story without telling too much.
Why Children Need This Strategy	Retelling helps readers recall what is happening in the story, develop a sense of story structure, and become more accurate in monitoring their understanding. They can transfer this knowledge of story structure to their own story writing.
Secret to Success	Think about what you are reading. Stop and reread if you can't remember. One way to teach students how to remember story sequence and character elements in the story is by using words such as *first*, *next*, *then*, *last*, and *finally*.
How We Teach It	Retelling is used on many beginning reading assessments, yet for years we never really taught students explicitly how to retell. We start by modeling this with our students during read-alouds. This technique is used by storytellers, and we borrowed the idea, giving our students a kinesthetic action to help them focus and remember the story. Introducing the Retell Rope, we hold up a small rope knotted eight times. Each knot represents one thought from the story. We also show the class a picture representation of the rope. We tell the class that when we come to each knot, it will remind us to state the next event from the story. We then read a story. After reading the story, we retell it using the rope and knots, stopping at each knot and telling an important fact from the story. Before our next story, we go to our visual of the rope and start labeling each knot to give students a structure for the retelling. Under each knot, we write the following words and explain them as we are writing: *Characters, Setting, Problem, Event 1, Event 2–Next, Event 3–Then, Event 4–Finally, Ending—Circle Back to Solve Problem* We then show the rope with both ends connecting to each other to demonstrate that the retelling ends by solving the problem in the beginning. Language we use: "Who were the main characters?" "What problem did the main characters experience?" "How was the problem solved?" "How did the story end?" "What happened first, next, and last?"
Troubleshooting	Listening to a student retell a story is also an assessment strategy. We listen as students reveal what they think is most important in the story. This gives us a window into the students' thinking about story organization and their oral language development and vocabulary. We typically think of retelling a story as an oral activity. Keeping the retelling oral will support students who may have difficulty with this strategy, allowing them to focus on the story rather than their written response.

Ready Reference Form

<table>
<tr><td colspan="2">Goal: Comprehension   Strategy: Use Prior Knowledge to Connect with Text</td></tr>
<tr><td>Definition</td><td>Readers bring information from what they already know or what they have read before about a topic and connect it with what they are reading to increase their understanding of the text and to remember what they have read.</td></tr>
<tr><td>Why Children Need This Strategy</td><td>Using prior knowledge can help students connect their own experiences with the text to better understand and make sense of what they are reading. The term prior knowledge is also thought of as making connections.</td></tr>
<tr><td>Secret to Success</td><td>Pause before and during the reading of the text to relate what is being read in the story to what is already known.</td></tr>
<tr><td>How We Teach It</td><td>Using a grade-appropriate text, we model for students how we activate our prior knowledge before we begin reading, using some of the language below. As we provide guided practice, we ask students to "listen and talk" to their elbow buddy about the following:

Activate or think about your prior knowledge or connections you have to the text.
How did you feel in a similar situation?
How did these connections help you to better understand the story?

Language we use:
"What experiences have you had that might be similar to what this book cover is telling you?"<br>"What do you already know about this content, genre, or author?"<br>"While reading: Does this part of the story remind you of anything you have done before or read before that will help you understand this section of the story better?"<br>"Using what you already knew about the topic, did that information help you understand this selection?"</td></tr>
<tr><td>Troubleshooting</td><td>Students pick up on using prior knowledge quickly, but at times the prior knowledge does not move them forward with deep understanding of the text. If this happens, we remind students that the goal of using prior knowledge is to connect us to the text for better understanding and retention of what we read.

We may take out a KWL chart (Know, Want to know, Learned) and fill it out with students, coaching them through the process of drawing on their background knowledge and connecting it to the text.</td></tr>
</table>

Ready Reference Form

Goal: Comprehension	**Strategy: Make a Picture or Mental Image**
Definition	When students listen to or read text, they can create pictures in their mind or make a mind movie. When readers visualize what is happening in the story, they remember more of what they read or hear.
Why Children Need This Strategy	Making a picture or mental image assists readers in understanding what they read by creating images in their mind, based on the details in the text and their prior knowledge.
Secret to Success	Readers put themselves in the story or text by making a mind movie. They also identify details that help them make pictures in their minds.
How We Teach It	When teaching students to make pictures in their mind before, during, and after reading, we start by explaining how pictures help students remember what they are reading: ◆ by thinking about what they know about the text before they read; ◆ by using sensory details to create mental pictures; ◆ by looking back at the pictures in their brains after the story to remember what has happened. We then model how we make pictures in our mind and ask students to do the same during our read-aloud, with partners and independently. Some language we use: "What do you see in your mind as I read this selection?" "Take the information I am reading and make it into a movie. Pretend you are at the theater and watching the story." "Can you see yourself in this selection?"
Troubleshooting	If students have a difficult time making pictures in their minds, we say, "If you could see a picture in your mind, what would it look like?" This simple rewording helps students bridge what they think they should be doing with creating the pictures. Other language we use to guide readers: Which details helped create a picture in your mind? Before you begin the story, make a picture in your mind of what you have seen before that may be in the selection.

Ready Reference Form

Goal: Comprehension	Strategy: Ask Questions Throughout the Reading Process
Definition	Readers are actively involved in reading by asking themselves questions before, during, and after reading a selection, thus increasing their comprehension of the material.
Why Children Need This Strategy	Readers who ask questions during reading are actively engaged and thus tend to remember important details and information. While asking questions, readers are monitoring their comprehension.
Secret to Success	Readers must be able to generate their own questions. Not all questions will be answered.
How We Teach It	When introducing this strategy in a whole-group format, we begin by explaining that asking questions during the reading process can help us focus on what we are reading, can give us a purpose for reading, and enables us to monitor our reading or check to see whether we are understanding what we are reading. We model this questioning process by stopping during our reading and stating the question we have in our minds. We model for a few days and then ask students to participate while we are reading aloud by turning and talking. Finally, we have students practice asking questions independently. Questions we may use while reading: "What does this mean?" "Is this important?" "How do I think this story will end?" "What will this selection be about?" "What does this word mean?" "What did I learn?" "Do I need to read this again?"
Troubleshooting	If children have difficulty asking questions, we step back and teach them different kinds of questions readers ask. One resource we have found useful is Taffy Raphael's (2006) work on QAR (Question, Answer, Relationship). She has defined questions under four categories: Right There, Think and Search, Author and Me, On My Own. Using these categories and her definitions under each can make asking questions more concrete and attainable.

Ready Reference Form

Goal: Comprehension	Strategy: Predict What Will Happen; Use Text to Confirm
Definition	To predict, readers tell what they think will happen in the story; to confirm, readers find out whether their predictions were true, partially true, or way off.
Why Children Need This Strategy	Using this strategy helps readers make connections to the text, think ahead, and become more engaged.
Secret to Success	Readers follow three steps: 1. Look at the details in the selection. 2. Decide what they think will happen next based on the details and background knowledge. 3. Look back and check to make sure the prediction was accurate (confirm).
How We Teach It	After defining the strategy for the class, we model its use in the whole group. As we move to guided practice, we give students a piece of text (fiction or nonfiction) and pair them. We ask them to look at the text and predict what will happen, then partner-read the selection and find places in the text that can confirm whether their predictions were true, partially true, or way off. If the predictions were way off, we ask the pairs to go back and change their prediction to be true. Language we use: "What do you think will happen based on your information?" "What clues are you using to state that prediction?" "What kind of clues did you use? Pictures, words, or background knowledge?"
Troubleshooting	Predicting is a strategy most readers do quite well. The difficulty is with making predictions that have something to do with the story or selection. Our youngest readers tend to make unsubstantiated predictions that do not deepen their thinking about what is happening in the text. Asking them to confirm predictions with the text helps students comprehend what is happening further ahead.

Ready Reference Form

Goal: Comprehension	**Strategy: Infer and Support with Evidence**
Definition	Readers figure out what the author is saying even though it might not be written down. Using their background knowledge, clues from the text, illustrations, and captions, the reader makes meaning of the selection.
Why Children Need This Strategy	Not all authors tell the reader everything they want you to know in the selection. Students learn to be detectives by looking for clues or evidence in the text to figure out the meaning of the selection.
Secret to Success	There may be a bit of guessing involved when inferring. Readers will need to use everything they already know and clues from the text, illustrations, and captions to figure out or guess what is happening.
How We Teach It	As always, the most effective way we teach any strategy is by modeling our thinking out loud and labeling it for our students. One of our first lessons for inferring is the Inferring Game. For a full description of the lesson, see page 100. As students become more skilled with the game, we use a favorite picture book and start anchoring the practice they have had with inferring in statements as part of the Inferring Game, our read-alouds, and their own books.
Troubleshooting	At times students make wild inferences and we wonder how to move them to grounding their thinking in meaning by taking them back to articulating the clues they find or the evidence. We slow students down by asking them to write their clues or evidence on a sticky note. During our small-group meetings and individual conferences, we monitor their progress. For an example of a small-group strategy lesson using this strategy, see page 100.

Ready Reference Form

Goal: Comprehension	Strategy: Use Text Features (Titles, Headings, Captions, Graphic Features)
Definition	Nonfiction text contains common features such as titles, headings and subheadings, captions, maps, diagrams, charts and graphs, legends, bold and italicized text, glossaries, indexes, and cutaways. Readers recognize and use these features to help them understand what they are reading.
Why Children Need This Strategy	When students read nonfiction material, they will encounter text features that are not evident when reading fiction. Students who have had experience and know the components and functions of text features improve their comprehension of the text.
Secret to Success	Understand that most nonfiction will have text features. Tune in to these features, and use your background knowledge about them and how they aid in comprehension.
How We Teach It	Our favorite way to teach this strategy involves using clear acetate sheets and markers. Laying the acetate sheet over the text allows for writing, circling, and marking text features with a water-soluble marker, without writing on the text itself. This highly visual approach allows us to point out to children the features and write our thinking rather than just explaining what the features are. Once we show kids how to use these tools, we send them off with partners or by themselves to work with text features in a similar manner. This activity helps train a student's eyes to look at the features of text before, during, and after they read a passage or article.
Troubleshooting	Many students think they need to delve right into a piece of text. It takes modeling, time, and encouragement to teach children that using text features is an appropriate strategy as well as a perfectly acceptable way to gain more information as they comprehend what they read. For an example of this strategy, see page 119.

Ready Reference Form

Goal: Comprehension	Strategy: Summarize Text; Include Sequence of Main Events
Definition	Summarizing is taking selections of text and reducing them to their bare essentials: the gist, the key ideas, and the main points that are worth noting and remembering.
Why Children Need This Strategy	The reader captures the most important parts of text but expresses them in a shorter version so the text is more easily remembered. As readers we need to absorb the meaning of the passage and then capture in our own words the most important elements from the original so we can remember, organize, and understand the importance of what we have read.
Secret to Success	Readers are able to articulate the main point of a selection. At times finding key words or phrases may be helpful to support their ideas.
How We Teach It	During our chapter book read-aloud, we begin modeling how to summarize. Before we begin the second chapter, we summarize what happened in the previous chapter, stating the main ideas and using story elements to organize the summary. We model discerning important or nonimportant information that we would include in our summary. After we make a few attempts alone, we work together with students to identify the main ideas in the previous chapters. In primary classes, we institute an artist of the day, who draws or paints a picture of the most important information from the chapter just read. We meet with the child to write the main ideas they drew or painted, finally compiling a class book summarizing the read-aloud. This book becomes the anchor we refer to when speaking about summaries. With older students we model writing summaries of the chapters from our class read-aloud, modeling our thinking as we decide what is important and worth noting and what details we will leave out because of their relative insignificance to the story. Once we think students understand how to write a summary, this becomes a weekly expectation and part of their response journal that is graded. Language we use: "What is this selection about?" "What are the main ideas of this selection? What is your evidence?" "What is not important to remember in this selection? Why?"
Troubleshooting	Summarizing is often used but is challenging for many of our students. If it does pose a challenge, many times it is because students are trying to retell the whole story with great detail and don't know how to cut it down to the most critical elements. This is when we step in with more modeling either with the whole group, in small groups, or one on one, depending on the number of students who need the strategy. For an example of an individual conferring lesson using this strategy, see pages 78 and 101.

Ready Reference Form

Goal: Comprehension	**Strategy: Use Main Idea and Supporting Details to Determine Importance**
Definition	Readers understand the most important idea about what is being read. This idea is often stated in a sentence in the passage, whereas other sentences comprise pieces of information that tell more about the most important idea.
Why Children Need This Strategy	Identifying and understanding main ideas along with determining importance are prerequisite skills to summarizing text. Readers summarize the most important aspects of the text by determining the details that are significant and discard those that are not while stating the main idea in their own words, thus improving comprehension and understanding what is read.
Secret to Success	When constructing the main idea of a piece of text, the reader may start with a topic they think the selection is about and then add one detail to support it.
How We Teach It	Many students shy away from the main idea because they confuse it with theme or topic. To clarify more completely, we start by establishing a common language as we teach and review with our students the following terms: *topic, main idea, theme*, and *supporting details*. We find that when students understand these terms, we are on the right path to understanding main idea. We then model this process of determining the main idea, pointing out that one person's view of the author's main idea may be different from another. When we determine the main idea, we always support our claim with evidence from the text. The terms: The **topic** is the subject, or what the text is about. The **main idea** is the most important idea about the topic and is expressed as a sentence or two. When we identify the main idea, it is usually in a sentence; if we say just a word, we are probably referring only to the topic. A **theme** is the big idea from the text. This is often an idea or lesson the author wants the reader to know from reading the text. **Supporting details** are bits of information that are used to verify and support the main idea. Language we use: "In a few words, what is this selection about?" "What would you say is the most important idea about this topic?" "Did you find the main idea stated in the passage or did you have to infer it?"
Troubleshooting	If the main idea is not stated in a sentence in the passage, the reader must infer the main idea based on the details and their prior knowledge of the topic and what they learn from the text. We are clear with students that this process of determining the main idea can require considerable thinking and hard work. To support students who need scaffolding for this strategy, we may meet every day for a week, checking in on them and asking them each time to identify the main idea and support their thinking with details from the text.

Ready Reference Form

Goal: Comprehension	Strategy: Determine and Analyze Author's Purpose and Support with Text
Definition	Identify why the author wrote a text, by giving specific examples from the text to support the reader's inference; deepens understanding for how to read and comprehend the text.
Why Children Need This Strategy	Readers infer the meaning of text based on the author's purpose for writing it, which may be to persuade, to inform, or to entertain, to name a few.
Secret to Success	Discovering and identifying the clues to determine what the reader thinks the author's purpose is for writing the selection helps the reader infer the meaning and decide how to approach the text. Authors usually don't tell readers why they wrote their selections; the readers have to figure that out and give evidence from the text to support their thinking.
How We Teach It	We model this strategy, asking ourselves before we start reading a selection some of the questions below. For the next week, each time we pick up any reading material, we ask the students to predict what the author's purpose is. We make an anchor chart with these three author's purposes: Persuade, Inform, and Entertain. We know authors may have other purposes, but we start with these three. Under each heading, we construct a list of descriptors or clues we are discovering for each purpose. Once we have a few descriptors under each heading, we begin by asking students to identify the author's purpose for books they are reading. We constantly ask students to support their beliefs by giving specific examples from the text that give evidence to their conclusions. Language we use: "Do I know anything about this author?" "Is this selection going to teach me something, make me laugh, or try to get me to do something?" "What clues can I find in the text that support what I think?" "Infer why you think the author wrote this text." "How might you approach reading this text, knowing the author's purpose?" "After reading the selection, do you still agree with your inference about why the author wrote this text? If not, what do you think is the author's purpose now? What is your evidence?"
Troubleshooting	The students who need extra support in this area usually need practice predicting author's purpose. Often they don't have enough information to discern the different reasons authors write text and then to support their opinion with details from the selection. We put these students on our conferring calendar and check in daily. We bring a different book to each conference and ask them, "What is the author's purpose for writing this text? What makes you think this?" Going through this process individually will support the students and give them daily practice until we believe they have the skills to identify purpose and why it is important to their reading.

Ready Reference Form

Goal: Comprehension	Strategy: Recognize Literary Elements (Genre, Plot, Character, Setting, Problem/Resolution, Theme)
Definition	Readers identify common elements of a story as they read that include plot, character, setting, and theme. Using these elements helps readers infer what will happen next.
Why Children Need This Strategy	Identifying and understanding the main literary elements of a story such as character, setting, plot, and problem/resolution gives readers a process for storing information to remember and to comprehend what the story is about. This knowledge will also help students as they are writing stories.
Secret to Success	Literary elements work together to form and enhance the story. We learn literary elements separately, and then combine them in our mind for better understanding of the story.
How We Teach It	Teaching literary elements does not happen in one day, or even in one week. We start by teaching our youngest learners about these elements, revisiting these lessons over the years. It is helpful to know the most common elements. **Literary Elements** **Characters:** Who or what the story is about, based on the actions or words used. **Plot:** The important events in the story, which include the *conflict*, or *problem*, of the story, and *resolution*, or how the problem was solved. **Setting:** Where and when the story occurs. The author may also convey mood through the setting, leading the reader to feel a certain way, such as sad, scared, or happy. **Theme:** The underlying message, or meaning, of the story. This can be stated or inferred. There are many other literary elements that add to a unified story, such as foreshadowing, flashback, point of view, irony, symbolism, and figurative language (to name a few). We start with the most common elements as stated above, and add others as students become more sophisticated readers. Through our read-alouds and thinking aloud, we identify each of the elements of the story. We begin with basic understanding of the elements, and then move to deeper thinking to not just identify each element, but to start using them together to enhance our comprehension. For example, the questions below are more sophisticated than the beginning questions such as "Who are the characters?" Now we think about how the characters have changed during the story, giving examples and saying why we came to that decision. Language we use: "Does the character change during the story? Give examples." "What is the setting in the story? Is it stated or do you have to infer?" "How is the mood described in the story based on the setting?" "What is the problem of the story? Give text evidence to support this." "How has the problem been resolved? Support your thinking."
Troubleshooting	As readers encounter more sophisticated text, they need to be taught and exposed to other literary elements to understand stories more completely. Ask the students to tell you how they determined the literary elements in the story by giving details from the story to support their thinking. A graphic organizer such as a story map can help students visually organize a story's elements.

Ready Reference Form

Goal: Comprehension	**Strategy: Recognize and Explain Cause-and-Effect Relationships**
Definition	Readers understand that in-text events happen (effects), along with the reason why they happen (causes). When students recognize this relationship, comprehension is increased.
Why Children Need This Strategy	The cause-and-effect relationship is a basic thinking skill and text structure for all types of reading and subject areas. Students use the understanding of this relationship in social studies, science, all school subjects, and day-to-day living, whether watching TV, playing games, or in friendships.
Secret to Success	Look for clue words that will signal what happened and why it happened.
How We Teach It	Some clue words may include *because, if, then, since, so, therefore, as a result of.* Explain the importance of cause and effect and how an author may structure and organize a section of the text using the cause-and-effect pattern. Show examples of this in the reading of a text. Through guided practice we ask students to identify the cause-and-effect relationship in different selections we read. At times we must infer the cause, since it is not always stated. If this is the case, we ask ourselves, "Why do I think this happened?" or "Why might this have happened?" Language we use: "What happened and why did it happen?" "What were the clue words?" "Why would this have happened?" "Give examples of cause-and-effect relationships throughout your life—in your family, in sports, and in your friendships."
Troubleshooting	Sometimes the causes are not stated, which makes it difficult for our more literal learners to figure out a cause-and-effect relationship. Therefore, we meet with students individually and generate a possible list of effects together. We then embed this in reading by asking the students to keep track of any cause-and-effect relationships they find in their reading or conversations at home. The more we practice this with students, the more easily they can identify stated causes or inferred causes.

Ready Reference Form

Goal: Comprehension	Strategy: Compare and Contrast Within and Between Text
Definition	Readers understand new ideas in text by thinking about how things are alike or different, thus deepening their comprehension.
Why Children Need This Strategy	Comparing and contrasting text assists the reader by engaging them in thinking critically. Readers go beyond descriptions, summaries, or retells and gain a deeper understanding of what they are comparing or contrasting.
Secret to Success	Remember that comparing involves articulating likenesses and differences, whereas contrasting focuses only on differences.
How We Teach It	We begin by defining and giving examples of how to compare, by telling likenesses and differences of what we might be comparing. We may use two students and point out their similarities and differences. Then we compare characters in a story or settings. We always use a Venn diagram when teaching our students the idea of comparing and contrasting information. It is a great visual device that clearly shows this abstract concept. Teaching points to remember: Compare—tell how two or more things are alike and different clue words: *like, as* Simile—*than, as* Metaphor—no clue words Analogies—point out words with same relationship Contrast—tell how two or more things are different clue words: *but, unlike* Language we use: "How are these stories the same? How are they different?" "Compare the characters in each story." "How might you compare these stories?"
Troubleshooting	Help students understand the skill by relating it to classifying. When we are grouping things together, we classify them by likes and/or differences.

Ready Reference Form

Goal: Accuracy	**Strategy: Cross Checking . . . Do the Pictures and/or Words Look Right? Do They Sound Right? Do They Make Sense?**
Definition	Cross Checking is a strategy for ensuring the words (and sometimes pictures) make sense and match the letters on the page.
Why Children Need This Strategy	When what is read doesn't sound right or make sense. When students come to a word they don't know.
Secret to Success	Must be able to monitor for meaning and know when it is necessary to pause and fix up the meaning instead of just continuing to read. Constantly grounding reading in meaning is vital to the success of this strategy.
How We Teach It	We have found that the best way to teach this strategy is by guiding children to stop at the end of a sentence when what they read didn't make sense. We ask them to go back and find the word that was confusing. We give them highlighter tape or a special pointer to mark the word. We may also supply a sticky or even a clear acetate sheet and marking pen to lay over the text and circle the word. Once the word has been identified, we spend time teaching children the movements to go with Cross Checking: "Does the word I am reading match the letters written or the picture?" (Here they cross their right arm over their body so the right hand touches the left shoulder.) "Does it sound right?" (Left arm crosses over the body so the left hand touches their right shoulder.) Finally, "Does it make sense?" (Both arms come down with hands pointing to the ground.) By giving a kinesthetic motion to the strategy, children are more apt to remember the questions that go with it. Teaching and modeling this strategy over and over all year long so children get into the habit of using it will help them learn to become readers who self-monitor their reading by stopping when it doesn't make sense and cross checking. Language we use: "While reading, ask yourself, 'Do the picture and/or letters in the word match what I am saying? Does it sound right and does it make sense?'"
Troubleshooting	For this strategy to be viable for beginning readers, they must ◆ read pictures, ◆ know some letters and some sounds, ◆ know the location of the beginning of a word. For advanced readers to be successful with Cross Checking, they must ◆ understand decoding of word parts. If a child has difficulty with this strategy, break down the process: Stop when meaning breaks down. Look and say the letters, and the word chunks in words. Use picture support. Cross Checking is an accuracy strategy on the CAFE Menu but is also a comprehension strategy that supports children when meaning breaks down. This strategy is one of the first we teach once children have a command over the accuracy strategy Use the Picture. From the first few moments with text, students are asked to cross-check what they are reading, which requires them to constantly think and monitor meaning.

Ready Reference Form

Goal: Accuracy	Strategy: Use the Picture . . . Do the Words and Pictures Match?
Definition	Using illustrations, photos, graphs, maps, and charts to help gain meaning from text and confirm that the words being read make sense.
Why Children Need This Strategy	This is one of the first stages of prereading. Illustrations can provide hints to help students decode a word. Using the pictures also prepares students for the accuracy strategy of Cross Checking, as well as for using charts, graphs, photos, and captions when reading nonfiction texts in later years.
Secret to Success	Knowing that using the pictures within text is a viable and appropriate strategy for decoding words and gaining meaning, not "cheating."
How We Teach It	Starting the first day of school we teach the lesson Three Ways to Read a Book to our youngest readers, or ELL students who are not yet reading or are just beginning to read. We want to ground students with the knowledge that oftentimes photos or illustrations are a vital part of the reading experience and can help us figure out a word or words or gain meaning from the text. We model reading the pictures. Beginning reading books often have just a few words on a page, and the illustrations can give clear support for figuring out the words. Reading pictures, which includes graphs, maps, charts, and their captions, is a very powerful nonfiction reading strategy. Using pictures is also a strategy for more advanced students that will support those reading different curricular texts. Each time we read a book, we spend time modeling how we look at pictures, maps, and graphs. We talk about our thinking so students can hear our processing. We also model stopping while we read to look at the pictures to help us gain information.
Troubleshooting	Use the Picture is an accuracy strategy on the CAFE Menu, but it also is a beginning comprehension strategy, sending a clear message for our beginning readers and English language learners that we are always thinking about meaning when we look at any text. Use the Picture is required before we can ask students to try the powerful strategy Cross Checking.

Ready Reference Form

Goal: Accuracy	Strategy: Use Beginning and Ending Sounds
Definition	When reading a word, using the sounds at the beginning of the word as well as at the end of the word.
Why Children Need This Strategy	Often children will look at the beginning letter or letters and guess a word that may fit in the sentence without looking at the rest of the word. They may not even know there is an end to a word.
Secret to Success	Children must slow down enough to look at and pay attention to the end of the word. For beginning readers, they must know there is an end of the word. Cross checking the word they just read. Students must know letter sounds as well as the concept of beginning and end. It is helpful if they are also exposed to the Cross Checking strategy so they will be certain the word they are reading matches the letters.
How We Teach It	When we teach this strategy to beginning readers, we often use a shared text that might be a nursery rhyme, poem, or Big Book. We look at words within text and focus children's attention on the beginning and ending sounds. To focus their attention, we may use colored highlighter tape or pieces of colored acetate sheets and have students lay the colors over the beginning and ending letter of the words they are decoding. Repeating this process with kids over and over will raise their level of awareness, and slow them down so they pay careful attention to the beginning and ending sounds. Once children slow down to focus in on beginning and ending sounds, we help them read the word correctly by coaching them to end their decoding with "Did that make sense?" Language prompts we might use: "Did you look at the whole word?" "Did what you just read make sense?" "Remember to cross-check the word and be certain it matches what you are saying."
Troubleshooting	If children struggle with this strategy, continuing to look at the beginning and middle of a word and then guessing, we have them mark the page with a sticky note and write the word out, or have them write the word on a whiteboard. Slowing down to write the word can help focus their attention on the end sound. See page 116 for an extended lesson.

Ready Reference Form

Goal: Accuracy	**Strategy: Blend Sounds; Stretch and Reread**
Definition	Taking the individual sounds of letters or phonemes and blending them together to read a word accurately.
Why Children Need This Strategy	Beginning readers often learn their sounds in isolation. The leap from knowing letter sounds to reading words can be daunting. Taking the isolated sounds and blending them together can be a first step to becoming a reader for many children.
Secret to Success	As you are blending the sounds together, listen for a word you might have heard before. Students know letter sounds and possess phonemic awareness, phoneme blending, and segment onset and rime.
How We Teach It	One of our favorite ways to teach this strategy is to give students a large rubber band or any stretchy band at all. We write a simple consonant-vowel-consonant (CVC) word on the whiteboard or chart, then have them take their bands between two hands. They pull the band apart a bit with each sound in the word, stretching out both the band and the word. When they have said each sound and the band is taut, they move their hands and the band quickly back together, with the band springing back to its original state. They say the word quickly at the same time, thus blending the sounds together. Another activity for teaching how to blend sounds together is called Stretch and Read. Students take one button for each letter in a word, laying them in a row and pushing each button forward as they say the individual sound. After saying each sound, they use both hands to push the buttons together, saying the word quickly. One of the verbal prompts we use is this one: "Say each letter as you stretch them out, then put them together and say it fast."
Troubleshooting	This strategy works best for simple, easy-to-decode words such as CVC words. The ability to have phonological awareness and be able to pull words apart and push them together auditorially is a very important prerequisite to the success of this strategy.

Ready Reference Form

Goal: Accuracy	Strategy: Flip the Sound
Definition	Teach children to use their knowledge of letter sounds to decode words by trying out, or "flipping," the different sounds a letter can make until they hear a word they recognize and that makes sense.
Why Children Need This Strategy	Many words in the English language don't follow conventional phonics rules. Drawing upon knowledge of the variety of sounds a letter makes can sometimes help children decode a word that has a letter that varies from the traditional sound associated with it.
Secret to Success	Being aware when a word doesn't sound right or make sense. Knowing the multiple sounds a letter or letter combination can make. Being able to flip the sounds around and then rely on comprehension to see whether the new word sounds right and makes sense. This strategy works particularly well with vowel sounds.
How We Teach It	Our favorite way to teach this strategy is by using a kinesthetic motion to remind students to flip the sound when they come to a word they don't know. Whether teaching the whole class, a small group, or an individual, we follow the same pattern: We model the strategy by showing them a word that we read incorrectly. If we are working with an individual, we wait until they read a word incorrectly and get to the end of the sentence. Then we stop them to model the strategy of Flip the Sound on their missed word. When we model the strategy, we put our hand palm-down and flip it over and say, "I think I'll try flipping the sound." We find it very important to articulate for the students that while we are flipping the sounds in a word, we must listen to see whether we recognize the word. Common language we use in lessons with Flip the Sound: "Did the word you just read sound right?" "When you flip the sound, listen for a word that you recognize." "What other sound could that letter make?"
Troubleshooting	If a student is struggling with this strategy, having a partner give them a prompt that is the kinesthetic motion of flipping over their hand can be a quiet reminder to try the strategy. See pages 74, 77, and 91 for an extended lesson.

Ready Reference Form

Goal: Accuracy	**Strategy: Chunk Letters and Sounds Together**
Definition	Chunking letters and sounds together within a word to make decoding more efficient, rapid, and accurate.
Why Children Need This Strategy	For children to be able to understand what they read, they must be able to read the words rapidly as well as accurately. This frees children to focus their attention on the meaning of what they have read.
Secret to Success	Watch for familiar word patterns such as blends, digraphs, prefixes, suffixes, compound words, and small words within a word.
How We Teach It	This strategy is typically for students reading beyond the basic CVC level. Once they know the different sounds made by digraphs, blends, etc., we use different tools to help kids identify them in their reading. When working with a large chart or Big Book, we will use "frames" that outline the smaller word parts. These frames are everything from cardboard cut into a handheld magnifying-glass shape (sometimes complete with colored acetate glued in place of where the lens would be) to a large fly swatter with part of the middle cut out to form a frame that can be laid over a word, isolating the smaller chunk. When we are using a book as we confer with students, we teach them to use their fingers to mask off the chunks found in words, decoding those chunks first, then moving on to tackle the whole word. Slowing the process of looking for smaller parts in words helps train students' eyes to look rapidly for those chunks.
Troubleshooting	The prerequisite to this strategy is knowing and having experience with the variety of digraphs, blends, prefixes, and suffixes found in words. Beginning with our youngest students, we spend time partaking in word studies that focus on these parts of words so as to build their background knowledge and experiences. Then as the words they encounter in text become more sophisticated, they have applicable knowledge and are ready to apply this strategy.

Ready Reference Form

Goal: Accuracy	Strategy: Skip the Word, Then Come Back
Definition	When students come to words they don't know, they skip over the word until they come to the end of the sentence or passage. Then readers back up and read the sentence again, using the first letter or letters of the skipped word and their context clues to decode the unknown word.
Why Children Need This Strategy	If we don't teach students how to skip a word and come back, some children will stall on the unknown word and be unable to move on. Using this strategy also allows readers to comprehend using context clues.
Secret to Success	Skip the unknown word, but be certain to come back. This strategy is a lead-in to Trade a Word.
How We Teach It	When introducing and practicing this strategy, our favorite way to teach begins with the use of shared text (Big Book, chart, or copy of text projected electronically on the wall or screen). Before displaying the text, we take sticky notes and cover up a word or two in a passage. We ask students to pretend the covered word is one they don't know. We model skipping over the unknown word, reading the rest of the sentence, and then backing up to reread the sentence. When we reread the sentence, we uncover the first letter of the sticky note–covered word and demonstrate how we use the first letter and the context clues within the passage to try to figure it out.
Troubleshooting	Help children realize it is okay to skip over a word and then come back to it.

Ready Reference Form

Goal: Accuracy	Strategy: Trade a Word/Guess a Word That Makes Sense
Definition	When readers encounter words they don't know, but they understand the gist of the text, they insert a word that makes sense in place of the unknown word.
Why Children Need This Strategy	This strategy provides the reader with the option to continue reading by using a similar word for an unknown word. Reading continues and meaning stays intact.
Secret to Success	Prerequisite strategy of Skip the Word, Then Come Back builds readers' confidence that even if they don't know every word, they have strategies to draw on. Readers must understand what they are reading so they can substitute a word that makes sense.
How We Teach It	Our favorite way to teach this strategy is very similar to Skip the Word, Then Come Back. We use shared text and a sticky note to cover a word or two within the text, except for the first letter, before showing the class. We model that when readers come to words they don't know, they can use the context clues and look at the first letter of the word, substituting a word that would make sense in the story. Then the reader continues reading the sentence and clarifies that the substituted word holds the meaning of the passage. Language we use: "Look at the first letter or letters: what word would make sense in this sentence that begins with that letter's sounds?"
Troubleshooting	If students are having a difficult time with this strategy, reteach Skip the Word, Then Come Back. Double-check that readers know the sounds letters make.

Ready Reference Form

Goal: Fluency	Strategy: Voracious Reading
Definition	Readers become more fluent by increasing their volume of reading.
Why Children Need This Strategy	Most students develop fluent reading normally with little instructional guidance. Allington believes that children who come to school having heard hours and hours of reading become fluent readers naturally unless "something in the classroom instruction interferes." His research leads him to conclude that the "volume of reading matters critically in the development of fluent, proficient readers" (2009a, 100).
Secret to Success	Readers whose goal is to improve their fluency will spend hours each day reading "good-fit books" at school and, if possible, at home. When increasing students' fluency, the key to success is increasing the amount of time they read.
How We Teach It	Voracious Reading is also found under Expand Vocabulary strategies on the CAFE Menu. Many of the same principles of how to teach this strategy hold true. The difference between voracious reading for fluency work and voracious reading for vocabulary work is based on what the child needs. Our language for introducing it changes slightly, depending on the strategy, as we point out why voracious reading would help fluency or vocabulary. For fluency development, we might use the following language: "We are going to give you time each day to read. I have noticed that you are choosing books that are too hard for you to read. You are not able to practice your fluency, because you are spending so much time sounding words out and trying to figure out what the words mean. We are going to work together today to find a book that is a 'good fit' for you. When the book you choose is on your reading level and you are interested in it, you will be able to practice reading smoothly and with expression. You will understand what you are reading and ultimately improve your fluency." Creating a whole class of children who want to and do read requires the following: ◆ Reading to the students every day from a wide variety of materials, modeling a love of reading ◆ Providing time each day for the children to read material of their choice that is of high interest for the reader ◆ Providing ongoing support—matching children to texts based on interest and readability
Troubleshooting	Finding and carving out time during the day for all students to read, especially our students who need the voracious reading as a strategy, can be a challenge. With these students, we might add them to our conferring calendar every day for a week or two, to help them get in the habit of reading and being accountable. We will also be able to check in to make sure they are reading a good-fit book, which is a key for this strategy to succeed.

Ready Reference Form

Goal: Fluency	**Strategy: Read Appropriate-Level Texts That Are a Good Fit**
Definition	To foster fluency and comprehension, students are engaged in high accuracy or high success reading, so most of each student's independent reading time is spent with material they can read with 99–100 percent accuracy.
Why Children Need This Strategy	"In order to read fluently, all readers need texts that they can read with a high degree of accuracy and automaticity. When readers are provided with texts that are too difficult, fluent reading is impossible" (Allington 2009a, 26).
Secret to Success	Students have time to find a good fit, are given time to read the book during the school day, and have someone supporting them and holding them accountable.
How We Teach It	We teach this lesson the first day of school and review it often throughout the year. Many students will start picking "good-fit books" right away, whereas others may have difficulty choosing an appropriate-level book and need this reminder lesson the whole year through. We hold students accountable for reading good-fit books through our one-on-one conferring. It is here that we listen to children's reading to see whether they can follow the "I-Pick" method for choosing books. If not, we help them find the book that will engage them right then and there during our conference. While the I-Pick Method emphasizes K—Know most of the words, we also address the other four behaviors for choosing books, because it is these behaviors that will help students find a book they will stick with. We teach this good-fit lesson to our whole class by introducing the "I Pick" method from our book *The Daily Five: Fostering Literacy Independence in the Elementary Classroom* (2006). I—I pick a book P—Purpose—What is my purpose for choosing this book? I—Interest—Am I interested in this book? C—Comprehend—Do I understand what I just read? K—Know—Do I know most of the words? We might use language or prompts like the following: "Is that a good-fit book for you? Show me how you know that." "Let's go through your book box and you can show me your good-fit books."
Troubleshooting	We teach this lesson to the whole group on the first day of school, and on subsequent days and for weeks afterward to our transitional and fluent readers. For our beginning readers, we also introduce good-fit books, but we don't emphasize reading material with 99–100 percent accuracy. Children at this stage of reading are in text that may have one to eight words on a page. They may know only two of the words and are reading the pictures to support their meaning. They may also be retelling the story without even reading the words. These are all appropriate reading practices for our beginning readers. It isn't until students read more accurately that we expect them to choose and read books with 99–100 percent accuracy.

Ready Reference Form

Goal: Fluency	Strategy: Reread Text
Definition	Students reread a selection of text several times until they can read it smoothly, accurately, and with expression.
Why Children Need This Strategy	Children benefit from this rereading strategy because of the ease with which it can be implemented in the classroom. Students can reread by themselves or with a partner and with any "good-fit books" they are reading.
Secret to Success	For this strategy to improve fluency, students must read from a good-fit book. If students are choosing books that are too difficult, their cognitive demand and energy will be spent on decoding words, with little left for fluent reading.
How We Teach It	During our conferences, we set the purpose for the task of rereading to make reading smooth, accurate, and with expression, which will give the students a chance to practice their fluency. Students will ◆ choose a different paragraph from the story they are reading each day; ◆ reread that paragraph until they can read it smoothly, read it with expression, and read all the words correctly; ◆ eventually practice reading the same passage at a quicker pace. We tell students this practice doesn't take long—only about five to eight minutes of reading time each day, and with only one paragraph a day. They can practice this rereading strategy during Read to Self or Partner Read and also at home. We might use language or prompts like the following: "Which passage did you practice yesterday to increase your fluency?" "When did you practice this passage? Was it during Read to Someone or Read to Self?" "Let's try this together: show me the passage you are practicing today, and let me hear you read it." "Do you think you are becoming more fluent? How do you know?"
Troubleshooting	Rereading is a strategy used by even our youngest readers as they read the same text over and over to gain control of the words and meaning of the text. This very common strategy of rereading with our early readers changes from rereading to make sense of what is read to rereading paragraphs to practice fluency. We have never had a whole class of students who needed to work on their fluency. Consequently, we have never taught this particular lesson in a whole group. This is a specialized strategy we use with only a few of our students. For an example of this lesson, see pages 82–83.

Ready Reference Form

Goal: Fluency	**Strategy: Practice Common Sight Words and High-Frequency Words**
Definition	Children recognize at first sight the most commonly used English words found in reading. Many of these words are irregular words that do not follow a decoding rule or pattern. Once readers remember these words, they can read them quickly and understand what they read.
Why Children Need This Strategy	A very early stage of fluent reading is being able to read words by "sight." Knowing these words and reading them quickly will allow readers to understand what is being read.
Secret to Success	Readers will need to see and experience these words over and over again in isolation and embedded in text to remember them.
How We Teach It	We typically focus on sight-word learning in the following two ways: ◆ We introduce about five words each week to our whole class and spend the rest of the week making connections to these words, anchoring them to text, and finding them in our reading and around the room. ◆ Students practice these words during the word work rotation of Daily Five. Here they have many opportunities and modes in which to work with these words. Language we may use: "Look at that sentence. Do you see any sight words you recognize?" "Look on this page. Let's go through and identify all the sight words you know so far."
Troubleshooting	For kids who just can't seem to remember sight words, we do the following: ◆ Cut back the number until they are successful. ◆ Add more kinesthetic repetition and practice. ◆ Cycle back through the words to keep them fresh in their brain.

Ready Reference Form

Goal: Fluency	**Strategy: Adjust and Apply Different Reading Rates to Match Text**
Definition	Readers use a constant rate for most materials they read but learn to use different speeds based on the types of tasks and their purpose for reading.
Why Children Need This Strategy	Some readers have yet to learn how to adjust their reading rate or are unaware that other readers adjust their rate to match their purpose for reading. Because these readers read everything at the same rate, they struggle to complete and comprehend lengthy reading.
Secret to Success	Shift reading gears based on your purpose for reading and what you are reading.
How We Teach It	We typically begin teaching students about rate by using Carver's (1990) analogy of reading. He compares reading rate to shifting the gears on a car. We explain that the low gears are slow and powerful, whereas higher gears are speedy but are the least powerful. Just like moving fast or slow in a car, our reading rate changes depending on the purpose for our reading and what we are reading. When reading, we use ◆ our first gear, or slowest, most powerful gear, to memorize material; ◆ second gear to learn material; ◆ third gear for most of our reading; and ◆ fourth gear, our quickest speed, for skimming and scanning. Once students are aware of rate and Carver's analogy, we establish this common class vocabulary to talk about the rate at which we read. Teaching may sound like this: "What might be the rate you use to read this social studies text?" "Will you change your rate during this reading?" "What is your typical speed for reading your favorite chapter book?"
Troubleshooting	Teach students to be aware of their own reading rate. Students can learn to self-monitor, when to speed up and when to slow down, when they are audiotaped for reflection. We typically think of our slow readers and teaching them how to speed up. But it's just as difficult to help speedsters—we want them to shift into a slower gear.

Ready Reference Form

Goal: Fluency	**Strategy: Use Punctuation to Enhance Phrasing and Prosody (End Marks, Commas, etc.)**
Definition	Clustering words together by using our knowledge of the spoken patterns in the English language and using punctuation enhances our understanding of what we read.
Why Children Need This Strategy	Learning to read in phrases is important. The meaning of what is read is embedded in the chunk of words we read, not just in the isolated words themselves. The order and the way words are put together to make a sentence and then a paragraph create the meaning.
Secret to Success	Students must rely on their knowledge of phrasing from speaking English and transfer that knowledge to reading in phrases. Since most phrasing is learned early from the spoken language, we use the intonation and prosody we hear every day during our conversations with others. We then use similar voice patterns in reading, which enhances comprehension.
How We Teach It	With all of our fluency instruction, we begin with our read-alouds. We model and explain explicitly to students what fluency is, how it sounds, and why it is important. Before we even introduce phrasing, we start by cueing students into the intonation of our voice, showing them how we control our voice to go up and down. We then talk about how that affects what we are saying. This is usually anchored to Daily Five partner-reading, where we model the language we expect students to use when asking for a partner. We teach them that their voice rises at the end of the sentence "Do you want to be my partner?" We use our finger and draw a line showing how our voice follows a straight line, drops, and ends at a higher tone than when we started. We talk about how it feels if people end the statement with a lilt in their voice or if they drop it at the end. If a student doesn't naturally start using phrasing while reading, which most of them do, we often draw the phrase in a sentence, right under the words, using a scooping motion with our pencils to show all the words that are said together without a pause. We also point out any punctuation that helped us decide where the phrase was. Language we may use: "Did punctuation help you read that phrase of words?" "Show me by drawing in the phrases you will say here." "I am going to draw in this phrase; now I want you to say those four words together quickly. Let me show you what that sounds like." "Try saying those words together quickly—not word by word."
Troubleshooting	Most children learn and use phrasing if they have been reading "good-fit books." If there is an occasion where students are not phrasing, scooping the words together is a great first step.

Ready Reference Form

Goal: Expand Vocabulary	Strategy: Voracious Reading
Definition	Readers increase their vocabulary by reading and reading and reading.
Why Children Need This Strategy	"Reading is one of the major ways new words are learned" (Cunningham 2009, 16). Cunningham also says, "The number of words in your meaning vocabulary store is directly related to how much you read. Children who read the most have the biggest vocabularies. Children who read only when they are assigned something to read have smaller vocabularies" (2009, 15).
Secret to Success	Choosing a "good-fit book" and being motivated to stick with reading.
How We Teach It	Creating a whole class of children who want to read and do read requires the following: ◆ Reading to the students each and every day from a wide variety of materials, modeling a love of reading; ◆ Providing time each day for the children to read material of their choice and that have high interest for the reader; and ◆ Providing ongoing support, matching children to texts based on interest and readability.
Troubleshooting	Offering and maintaining a wide range and variety of material for students to choose to read can be the biggest challenge. Our most at-risk students typically have a narrow range of materials they are interested in, and making sure those materials are on a reading level students can access is difficult. In our schools, we are looking for resources, so each year all classroom teachers are given a small amount of money to buy books for our challenged readers, adding titles to classroom libraries that are specific to the students in their class that year.

Ready Reference Form

Goal: Expand Vocabulary	**Strategy: Tune In to Interesting Words and Use New Vocabulary in Speaking and Writing**
Definition	Students build word awareness and the understanding of words so they have "thinking power" left in their brain to comprehend and make meaning of what is read.
Why Children Need This Strategy	When students have at least six multiple exposures to a word in a variety of contexts, they develop significantly higher levels of comprehension (Block, Hasni, and Mangieri, 2005; National Reading Panel, 2000). Students who tune in to interesting words will encounter and remember new words, thus expanding their vocabulary.
Secret to Success	When students read independently, they must read and practice this strategy with a "good-fit book." Use a word collector for both whole-group lessons and individual conferences to record and remember the new words. For more on word collectors, see pages 84 and 152.
How We Teach It	This is one of the first strategies we teach to the whole class on the first day of school. We choose two or three words from our read-aloud that we think the children will encounter in their own reading or writing. ◆ While we are reading, we stop and make a big deal over one of the words, saying how much we love the sound of it. ◆ We write the word on the word collector under the first letter of the word (e.g., *deluge*, *d*). ◆ We continue reading until we come across two or three words each day. ◆ At the beginning of each literacy block, we review each of the words on the collector and discuss who has used it in their conversations or writing. Another tool we use to facilitate tuning in to interesting words is a table-talk notebook (see page 83).
Troubleshooting	We meet with the children in a one-on-one conference and discuss the words they are learning and using. This conversation helps deepen the understanding of words and comprehension of what they are reading. For examples of a one-on-one conference using this strategy, see pages 37, 84, and 102.

Ready Reference Form

Goal: Expand Vocabulary	Strategy: Use Pictures, Illustrations, and Diagrams
Definition	Readers increase their vocabulary by paying attention to pictures, illustrations, and diagrams. They use the context of the story, their background knowledge of what is being read, and at times infer to gain meaning of the word and text.
Why Children Need This Strategy	Illustrations give clues about the meaning of words and text. Paying attention to the pictures may confirm the meaning of words. Picture books are not the only texts where pictures convey meaning. Readers are exposed to pictures in much of their nonfiction reading. Knowing how to figure out words by using background knowledge, looking at the picture, and inferring its meaning enhances vocabulary.
Secret to Success	Cross checking: do the pictures match what I think the word means, and does it make sense?
How We Teach It	This strategy is used most often when working on the goal of accuracy. We teach students to "Use the picture . . . Do the words and pictures match?" by cross checking. During vocabulary work, we teach this strategy similarly, but now we focus on the word, writing it either on our whole-class word collector or in individual word collectors so we can learn it for later use. ◆ Read a picture book or nonfiction book. ◆ When you come to a word you don't know, stop. ◆ State the strategy you will use by telling students, "I am going to look at this picture to see if I can figure out what this word means." ◆ Infer meaning based on background knowledge of text and what is represented in the picture. ◆ Write the word on a word collector, or celebrate figuring out the word, which elevated your understanding of the text.
Troubleshooting	This is a pretty straightforward strategy. Teachers find when they are modeling their reading that it is natural to stop and review what they are thinking when they come to a word they don't know, looking at the pictures and then confirming meaning.

Ready Reference Form

Goal: Expand Vocabulary	**Strategy: Use Word Parts to Determine the Meaning of Words** (Compound Words, Prefixes, Suffixes, Origins, Abbreviations, etc.)
Definition	Use word parts to determine meaning of words (prefixes, suffixes, origins, abbreviations, etc.).
Why Children Need This Strategy	Looking at parts of words helps readers break the word's meaning apart and supplies them with a strategy to understand new words they encounter. While looking at the distinguishable parts of a word, readers use their background knowledge of the word parts along with their knowledge of the text to infer the meaning of the word.
Secret to Success	Each year children will learn many new words through direct, explicit instruction in their classrooms, but there is no way we can teach all the words students will encounter. This strategy gives readers a tool to figure out words they meet in their own reading.
How We Teach It	We usually introduce this strategy as a whole-class lesson, during word work, as we are talking about parts of words and their meaning. This is a great time to point out to students that we use our thinking about word parts to help us spell words and to enhance our understanding of words. We anchor this lesson to the CAFE Menu by putting up the strategy Use Word Parts to Determine the Meaning of Words. We spend a little time each day looking at word parts and patterns. We choose a word part and do the following: ◆ Introduce the word part (e.g., *un* or *tion*). ◆ Define the word part and how it affects the meaning of the word. ◆ Write examples of the word part in real words on an anchor chart. When introducing the prefix *un*, we would write *un* at the top of the anchor chart and add two words, *uninvited*, *unbelievable*. ◆ Discuss the meaning of each word and the effect *un* had on it. ◆ Infer what the meaning of the word is. ◆ Invite students to add their own words to the anchor chart that they encounter during this reading. ◆ Students read the sentence that contains the word they added to the anchor chart. ◆ Discuss the words students add and infer the meaning of the word and the sentence. The prompt we often use during our lessons is "Ask myself . . . Do I know any part of this word?"
Troubleshooting	As quickly as possible we anchor the words into text so students learn how to infer the meaning of words based on their parts. For examples of a small-group lesson using this strategy, see page 122.

Ready Reference Form

Goal: Expand Vocabulary	Strategy: Use Prior Knowledge and Context to Predict and Confirm Meaning
Definition	Context clues are the words, phrases, and sentences surrounding an unfamiliar word that give clues or hints to its meaning.
Why Children Need This Strategy	Students learn to use context clues to determine the meanings of words, but not all words can be figured out in this way. At times readers must piece together the meaning with the hints that are given, use the information they already have, and infer the meaning of the word.
Secret to Success	Knowing some of the clue words that are used as context words, such as *but, however, unlike, means, in other words, also known as*, etc., helps the reader figure out the meaning of the word. Punctuation may also provide clues to the meaning of a word.
How We Teach It	Learning specific types of context clues helps students use the information around the unknown word to infer its meaning. We teach students five types of context clues: synonym, definition, example, contrast, inference We introduce this strategy as a whole-group lesson. We explain the steps in figuring out the meaning of an unfamiliar word or phrase through the use of context clues. We teach the class these different context clues, what they mean, and how to use them with the steps below. When readers come to a word they don't know, they use this plan to check for context clues and to understand the text: ◆ Check for a context clue that is right there in the sentence. ◆ If readers find a context clue, they will reread the sentence with the new term or clue in mind. ◆ The students think to themselves what the sentence says using this context clue. ◆ If readers don't find a clue or understand the main point the author is making, they will have to try a different strategy to figure out the word, such as asking someone the meaning or using a dictionary.
Troubleshooting	If a student has a difficult time figuring out context clues, we step back and teach different "clue words" for each of the context clues. Students may also have difficulty self-monitoring. We layer on the accuracy strategy of Cross Checking, because many times they stumble on checking themselves to see whether what they are inferring looks right, sounds right, and makes sense. Cross Checking integrates comprehension and is a self-monitoring strategy.

Ready Reference Form

Goal: Expand Vocabulary	Strategy: Ask Someone to Define the Word for You
Definition	When readers have a question about the meaning of a word, they ask someone to tell them what the word means.
Why Children Need This Strategy	An easy way to get information about a word is to ask someone the meaning. This may be enough for many readers to get a sense of the general idea of the word. Knowing the gist of the word allows readers to get right back into the text for meaning to be preserved.
Secret to Success	Readers need someone close by to ask. The person needs to know the word and be able to define it for the reader. Most important, readers must then go back into the text and use all their knowledge to confirm the definition given.
How We Teach It	As with all of our instruction, we want students to have lots of strategies they can choose from for optimal learning, and this is a viable strategy. Many readers come to us knowing this strategy because it is easy. We broaden their knowledge of it by giving them a way to ask for help, and teach them that they must also work. We invite our students to ask one or all of these questions when they are asking for a definition: ◆ What is the word? ◆ What is the word like? ◆ What are some examples of this word being used in a sentence? This level of questioning will elicit a more complete definition, making it easier for them to self-assess: ◆ Go back to the text and substitute the definition that was given for the word. ◆ Read the selection again, using the definition. ◆ Does the definition of the word make sense in the sentence?
Troubleshooting	We used to think students needed to try to figure it out first. What we didn't see was that readers usually do try to figure it out first, quickly going through the variety of strategies they already know and then asking someone. As adults, if we have someone else in the room we trust, this is usually the second strategy we use. First we guess the meaning in our head, and then we ask someone to confirm or refute the meaning we inferred. Teaching children the added step of confirming the meaning helps them see this as a trustworthy strategy, but it also shows them they are involved in making meaning from the text.

Ready Reference Form

Goal: Expand Vocabulary	Strategy: Use Dictionaries, Thesauruses, and Glossaries as Tools
Definition	Readers use many word-learning tools to increase their understanding of words and texts they are reading.
Why Children Need This Strategy	Readers access word-learning tools when they need the precise definition of a word or definitions of other words that mean the same thing.
Secret to Success	Students need to know how word-learning tools work to use them successfully.
How We Teach It	We model and use the word-learning tools often during our whole-class read-alouds, or in content teaching. In a whole-class lesson, we regularly say, "Let's see what the dictionary says about this word; let's look it up on the computer today" or "What other word could the author have written? Let's check the thesaurus. I am going to put the thesaurus under the document camera and we'll figure out how we can find this word." Most of our work with word-learning tools is done in a light and positive way to promote their use.
Troubleshooting	When many of us think about vocabulary work with dictionaries, we think of the stereotypical example of students looking up words in the dictionary and copying down their meaning (and of course using them in sentences). We avoid this practice. Cunningham sums up current findings: "Copying and memorizing definitions has been and remains the most common vocabulary activity in schools. It is done at all levels and in all subjects. This definition copying and memorizing continues in spite of research that shows definitional approaches to vocabulary instruction increase children's ability to define words but have no effect on reading comprehension" (2009, 176).

Bibliography

Allen, J. 2000. *Yellow Brick Roads: Shared and Guided Paths to Independent Reading 4–12*. Portland, ME: Stenhouse.

———. 2004. *Tools for Teaching Content Literacy.* Portland, ME: Stenhouse.

Allington, R. L. 2001. *What Really Matters for Struggling Readers: Designing Research-Based Programs*. New York: Addison-Wesley Longman.

———. 2009a. *What Really Matters in Response in Fluency Research-Based Design Practices Across the Curriculum*. New York: Longman.

———. 2009b. *What Really Matters in Response to Intervention Research-Based Design*. New York: Longman.

Allington, R. L., and P. Johnston. 2002. *Reading to Learn: Lessons from Exemplary Fourth-Grade Classrooms*. New York: Guilford Press.

Atwell, N. 1987. *In the Middle: Writing, Reading, and Learning with Adolescents*. Portsmouth, NH: Heinemann.

———. 2007. *The Reading Zone: How to Help Kids Become Skilled Passionate, Habitual Critical Readers*. New York: Scholastic.

Beaver, J. 1997. *Developmental Reading Assessment (DRA)*. Parsippany, NJ: Pearson Education.

Beck, I. L. 2006. *Making Sense of Phonics: The Hows and Whys*. New York: Guilford Press.

Beers, K. 2002. *When Kids Can't Read, What Teachers Can Do: A Guide for Teachers 6–12*. Portsmouth, NH: Heinemann.

Betts, E. 1946. *Foundations of Reading Instruction*. New York: American Book Co.

Block, C. C., J. Hasni, and J. N. Mangieri. 2005. "Effects of Direct Vocabulary Instruction on Students' Vocabulary, Comprehension, and Affective Development." Paper presented at the annual meeting of the National Reading Conference, Miami.

Block, C. C., and M. Pressley. 2002. *Comprehension Instruction: Research-Based Best Practices*. New York: Guilford Press.

Boushey, G., and J. Moser. 2006. *The Daily Five: Fostering Literacy Independence in the Elementary Grades*. Portland, ME: Stenhouse.

———. 2007. *Good-Fit Books*. DVD. Produced by Choice Literacy. Portland, ME: Stenhouse.

Brand, M. 2004. *Word Savvy: Integrated Vocabulary, Spelling, and Word Study Grades 3–6*. Portland, ME: Stenhouse.

Bridges, W. 2003. *Managing Transitions: Making the Most of Change*. Cambridge, MA: DaCapo Press.

Buckner, A. 2005. *Notebook Know-How: Strategies for the Writer's Notebook*. Portland, ME: Stenhouse.

Burns, P., and B. Roe. 2002. *Informal Reading Inventory: Preprimer to Twelfth Grade*. Boston: Houghton Mifflin.

Calkins, L., A. Hartman, and Z. R. White. 2005. *One to One: The Art of Conferring with Young Writers*. Portsmouth, NH: Heinemann.

Cambourne, B., and J. Turbill. 1987. *Coping with Chaos*. Portsmouth, NH: Heinemann.

Carver, R. P. 1990. *Reading Rate: A Review of Research and Theory*. Boston: Academic Press.

Cole, A. D. 2004. *When Reading Begins: The Teacher's Role in Decoding, Comprehending, and Fluency*. Portsmouth, NH: Heinemann.

Collins, K. 2004. *Growing Readers: Units of Study in the Primary Classroom*. Portland, ME: Stenhouse.

Connor, C. M. 2007. "Learning Environments Underlying Literacy Acquisition." *Encyclopedia of Language and Literacy Development*. Available online at http://www.literacyencyclopedia.ca/index.php?fa=items.show&topicId=233.

Cunningham, P. M. 2009. *What Really Matters in Vocabulary Research-Based Practices Across the Curriculum*. New York: Longman.

Fink, R. 2006. *Why Jane and John Couldn't Read—And How They Learned: A New Look at Striving Readers*. Newark, DE: International Reading Association.

Fountas, I., and G. S. Pinnell. 2001. *Guiding Readers and Writers Grades 3–6: Teaching Comprehension, Genre, and Content Literacy*. Portsmouth, NH: Heinemann.

———. 2006. *Teaching for Comprehending and Fluency: Thinking, Talking, and Writing About Reading, K–8*. Portsmouth, NH: Heinemann.

Gambrell, L. B., L. M. Morrow, and M. Pressley. 2007. *The Best Practices in Literacy Instruction*. New York: Guilford Press.

Grinder, M. 1991. *Righting the Educational Conveyor Belt*. Portland, OR: Metamorphous Press.

———. 1995. *ENVoY: Your Personal Guide to Classroom Management*. Battle Ground, WA: Michael Grinder and Associates.

Hall, S. L., and L. C. Moats. 1999. *Straight Talk About Reading: How Parents Can Make a Difference During the Early Years*. Chicago: Contemporary Books.

Harvey, S., and A. Goudvis. 2000. *Strategies That Work: Teaching Comprehension to Enhance Understanding*. Portland, ME: Stenhouse.

Healy, J. 1994. *Your Child's Growing Mind: A Practical Guide to Brain Development and Learning from Birth to Adolescence*. New York: Doubleday.

Johnston, P. H. 2000. *Running Records: A Self-Tutoring Guide*. Portland, ME: Stenhouse.

———. 2004. *Choice Words: How Our Language Affects Children's Learning*. Portland, ME: Stenhouse.

Johnston, P. H., R. L. Allington, and P. Afflerbach. 1985. "The Congruence of Classroom and Remedial Reading Instruction." *Elementary School Journal* 85: 465–478.

Keene, E. O., and S. Zimmermann. 1997. *Mosaic of Thought: Teaching Comprehension in a Reader's Workshop*. Portsmouth, NH: Heinemann.

Krashen, S. 2004. *The Power of Reading: Insights from the Research*. Portsmouth, NH: Heinemann.

Kuhn, M. R. 2005. "A Comparative Study of Small Group Fluency Instruction." *Reading Psychology* 26 (2): 127–146.

Kuhn, M. R., P. Schwanenflugel, R. D. Morris, M. Morrow, D. Woo, B. Meisinger, et al. 2006. "Teaching Children to Become Fluent and Automatic Readers." *Journal of Literacy Research* 38 (4): 257–388.

McGill-Franzen, A. M., and R. L. Allington. 2008. "Got Books?" *Educational Leadership* 65 (7): 20–23.

Mere, C. 2005. *More Than Guided Reading: Finding the Right Instructional Mix, K–3*. Portland, ME: Stenhouse.

Miller, D. 2002. *Reading with Meaning: Teaching Comprehension in the Primary Grades*. Portland, ME: Stenhouse.

———. 2008. *Teaching with Intention: Defining Beliefs, Aligning Practice, Taking Action, Grades K–5*. Portland, ME: Stenhouse.

Mooney, M. 1990. *Reading To, With and By Children*. Katonah, NY: Richard C. Owen.

Morrow, L. M., L. Gambrell, and M. Pressley. 2003. *Best Practices in Literacy Instruction*. New York: Guilford Press.

National Reading Panel. 2000. *Report of the National Reading Panel Subgroups: Teaching Children to Read*. Washington, DC: Government Printing Office.

Owocki, G. 2003. *Comprehension: Strategic Instruction for K–3 Students*. Portsmouth, NH: Heinemann.

Pearson, P. D., and M. C. Gallagher. 1983. "The Instruction of Reading Comprehension." *Contemporary Educational Psychology* 8: 317–344.

Pressley, M., R. Allington, R. Wharton-McDonald, C. C. Block, and L. M. Morrow. 2001. *Learning to Read: Lessons from Exemplary First-Grade Classrooms*. New York: Guilford Press.

Raphael, T. E., K. Highfield, and K. Au. 2006. *QAR Now: A Powerful and Practical Framework That Develops Comprehension and Higher-Level Thinking in All Students*. New York: Scholastic.

Routman, R. 2003. *Reading Essentials: The Specifics You Need to Teach Reading Well*. Portsmouth, NH: Heinemann.

Shaywitz, S. M. D. 2003. *Overcoming Dyslexia*. New York: Alfred Knopf.

Sibberson, F., and K. Szymusiak. 2003. *Still Learning to Read: Teaching Students in Grades 3–6*. Portland, ME: Stenhouse.

———. 2008. *Day-to-Day Assessment in the Reading Workshop: Making Informed Instructional Decisions in Grades 3–6*. New York: Scholastic.

Stiggins, R., J. Arter, J. Chappuis, and S. Chappuis. 2006. *Classroom Assessment for Student Learning: Doing It Right—Using It Well*. Portland, OR: Educational Testing Service.

Strickland, K. 2005. *What's After Assessment? Follow-Up Instruction for Phonics, Fluency, and Comprehension*. Portsmouth, NH: Heinemann.

Taberski, S. 1995. *A Close-Up Look at Teaching Reading: Focusing on Children and Our Goals*. Portsmouth, NH: Heinemann.

Taylor, B. M., P. D. Pearson, K. Clark, and S. Walpole. 2000. "Effective Schools and Accomplished Teachers: Lessons About Primary Grade Reading Instruction in Low-Income Schools." *Elementary School Journal* 101 (2): 121–166.

Tomlinson, C., and J. McTighe. 2006. *Integrating Differentiated Instruction and Understanding by Design: Connecting Content and Kids*. Alexandria, VA: Association for Supervision and Curriculum Development.

Tovani, C. 2006. *I Read It, but I Don't Get It: Comprehension Strategies for Adolescent Readers*. Portland, ME: Stenhouse.

Index

Page numbers followed by an *f* indicate figures.

O

P

R

S

U

V

W